DYMOND'S CAPITAL TRANSFER TAX

CONTENTS

DYMOND'S CAPITAL TRANSFER TAX

SECOND EDITION

SECOND CUMULATIVE SUPPLEMENT

BY

ROY R. GREENFIELD, LL.B. (Lond.)

Formerly Deputy Controller of the Capital Taxes Office

Oyez Longman

OYEZ LONGMAN PUBLISHING LIMITED
21-27 LAMB'S CONDUIT STREET
LONDON WC1N 3NJ

ISBN 0 85120 9254

Second Edition 1983
First Supplement 1984
Second Cumulative Supplement 1984

Printed in Great Britain by
Biddles Ltd, Guildford, Surrey.

PREFACE

Since the first supplement to the Second Edition of *Dymond's Capital Transfer Tax* was published, the law has been consolidated by the Capital Transfer Tax Act 1984 ('the CTT Act'), which comes into force on 1 January 1985. The Act does not change the law in any way, but it repeals all the relevant provisions of the Finance Acts from 1975 to 1984. So the Second Edition, which is not yet two years old, will need replacement much earlier than had been hoped. The Third Edition, incorporating the new statutory references, is now in preparation and will be published as soon as reasonably possible.

In the meantime, the present supplement states the law and practice at 31 July 1984. If readers have any difficulty in discovering where a particular section of the CTT Act is dealt with in *Dymond*, they can refer to the Table of Derivations printed at pp xxi–xxxvii below. This will show the corresponding section or paragraph of the old legislation, which can then be traced by reference to the Tables of Statutes at pp xlvii–xcix of the Second Edition and at pp ix–xvii below.

By far the most important change made by Part III of the Finance Act 1984 is the introduction of new scales of rates, by which—

(*a*) the rate bands are increased in line with inflation, so that the £60,000 threshold becomes £64,000;

(*b*) the top rate of tax on death is reduced from 75 per cent to 60 per cent and applies to values of £285,000 and upwards;

(*c*) the lifetime rates have become half the death rates all along the scale.

These are welcome improvements. *Dymond* has long argued that the rates of tax were too high and that there were too many exemptions and reliefs; and in the debate on the Finance Bill 1981 the Government confirmed that its objective was a tax regime of lower rates, greater simplicity and fewer reliefs. There has, however, been no reduction in the number of reliefs; rather have they been augmented by the extension of agricultural relief to stud farms. The relevant section was introduced rather hastily into the 1984 Act at the report stage and takes effect from 10 March 1981.

Out of all the new cases mentioned in this supplement, *Furniss* v *Dawson* (though not a CTT case) is the most important, as it reaffirms and clarifies the new approach of the House of Lords to tax avoidance schemes. In *IRC* v *Trustees of Sir John Aird's Settlement*

(No 2) the Court of Appeal upheld the decision of Nourse J that there is no such thing as a capital distribution or deemed distribution payment made before 13 March 1975; while in *Finch* v *IRC*, reversing Vinelott J, they decided that business relief was available before 1981 for settled property used in a life-tenant's business (so that FA 1981, s 100, may not have been necessary). On the other hand, it appears from *Minden Trust (Cayman) Ltd* v *IRC* that FA 1975, Sched 7, para 3(2A) *was* necessary (but that case is likely to go to appeal). *Moore* v *IRC* and *Swales* v *IRC*, both won by the taxpayer, were cases on the meaning of 'interest in possession'. The Revenue scored a solitary success in *IRC* v *Stannard*, which decided that an executor is personally liable for tax payable on the death of the testator. Other cases, not involving any point of Revenue law, were *Re Hogg* and *Stenhouse's Trustees* v *Lord Advocate*.

I acknowledge with gratitude the help received from Adrian Tytherleigh, of the Capital Taxes Office in London, and from Kathleen Patrick, of the Capital Taxes Office in Edinburgh. But, like the main volume, this supplement has no official authority and the views expressed are solely those of the author.

In this book, as in the statutes, the word 'tax' means Capital Transfer Tax unless the context otherwise requires. References to pages of Volume 1 of the Second Edition are shown in bold type.

3 September 1984 RRG

TABLE OF CASES

TABLE OF STATUTES

Page references in **bold** type indicate that the text has been reproduced.

TABLE OF STATUTORY INSTRUMENTS

Page references in **bold** type indicate that the text has been reproduced.

OECD MODEL CONVENTIONS

Page references in **bold** type indicate that the text has been reproduced.

CONVENTIONS AND DOUBLE TAXATION AGREEMENTS BETWEEN THE UNITED KINGDOM AND OTHER COUNTRIES

TABLE OF DERIVATIONS

Note: The following abbreviations are used in this Table:—

1975	= The Finance Act 1975 (c. 7)
1975 c. 21	= The Criminal Procedure (Scotland) Act 1975 (c. 21)
1976	= The Finance Act 1976 (c. 40)
1977	= The Finance Act 1977 (c. 36)
1978	= The Finance Act 1978 (c. 42)
1979 c. 14	= The Capital Gains Tax Act 1979 (c. 14)
1979 c. 46	= The Ancient Monuments and Archaeological Areas Act 1979 (c. 46)
1980	= The Finance Act 1980 (c. 48)
1980 c. 17	= The National Heritage Act 1980 (c. 17)
1981	= The Finance Act 1981 (c. 35)
1981 c. 54	= The Supreme Court Act 1981 (c. 54)
1981 c. 55	= The Armed Forces Act 1981 (c. 55)
1981 c. 61	= The British Nationality Act 1981 (c. 61)
1981 c. 66	= The Compulsory Purchase (Vesting Declaration) Act 1981 (c.66)
1982	= The Finance Act 1982 (c. 39)
1982 c. 48	= The Criminal Justice Act 1982 (c. 48)
1982 c. 50	= The Insurance Companies Act 1982 (c. 50)
1983	= The Finance Act 1983 (c. 28)
1983 (No. 2)	= The Finance (No. 2) Act 1983 (c. 49)
1983 c. 20	= The Mental Health Act 1983 (c. 20)
1984	= The Finance Act 1984 (c.)
S.I. 1979/927	= The Capital Transfer Tax (Northern Ireland Consequential Amendment) Order 1979
S.I. 1979/1575	= The Administration of Estates (Northern Ireland) Order 1979
S.I. 1982/1585	= The Capital Transfer Tax (Interest on Unpaid Tax) Order 1982
S.I. 1983/879	= The Transfer of Functions (Arts, Libraries and National Heritage) Order 1983
S.R. (N.I.) 1976/1980	= The Departments (Transfer of Functions) Order (Northern Ireland) 1976

Clause of Bill	Derivation
1	1975 s. 19(1).
2(1)(2)	1975 s. 20(5), (6).
(3)	5 s. 22(1).
(2)	1975 s. 22(9).

Clause of Bill	Derivation
5(1)(2)	1975 s. 23(1), (2).
(3)	1975 Sch. 10, para. 1(1); Sch. 21, para 16.
(4)	1975 s. 51(1), Sch. 10, para. 1(2).
(5)	1975 Sch. 10, para (13).
6(1)	1975 s. 24(2).
(2)	1975 Sch. 7, para. 3(1).
(3)	1975 Sch. 7, para. 5(1).
(4)	1975 Sch. 7, para. 6.
7(1)	1975 s. 37(1); 1981 s. 93(1); 1983 Sch. 9, para 3.
(2)(3)	1975 s. 37(2), (3).
8	1982 s. 91(1) to (4).
9	1980 s. 85(3); 1982 s. 91(5).
10(1)(2)	1975 s. 20(4).
(3)	1975 s. 20(4), (7); 1978 s. 74(1).
11	1975 s. 46.
12	1976 s. 89(1) to (5).
13(1)	1976 s. 90(1).
(2)	1976 s. 90(3); 1978 Sch. 11, para. 3(1).
(3)(4)	1976 s. 90(4); 1978 Sch. 11, para. 3(2).
(5)	1976 s. 90(5).
14	1976 s. 91(1), (2).
15	1976 s. 92(1).
16	1981 s. 97(1), (2).
17	1975 s. 47(1B), (3); 1976 ss. 121(1), 123(6); 1978 s. 68(1).
18(1)	1975 Sch. 6, para. 1(1); 1976 s. 94(2).
(2)	1975 Sch. 6, para. 1(2); 1976 s. 94(3); 1982 s. 92(1).
(3)	1975 Sch. 6, para. 15(1), (2).
(4)	1975 Sch. 6, para. 15(5).
19(1) to (3)	1975 Sch. 6, para. 2(1), (2); 1981 s. 94(1).
(4)	1975 Sch. 6, para. 2(3).
(5)	1975 Sch. 6, para. 8.
20(1)	1975 Sch. 6, para. 4(1); 1980 s. 86(3); 1981 s. 94(2).
(2)	1975 Sch. 6, para. 4(2).
(3)	1975 Sch. 6, para. 8.
21(1) to (4)	1975 Sch. 6, para. 5(1) to (3).
(5)	1975 Sch. 6, para. 8.
22(1) to (5)	1975 Sch. 6, para. 6.
(6)	1975 Sch. 6, para. 8.
23(1)	1975 Sch. 6, para. 10(1).
(2)	1975 Sch. 6, para. 15(1), (2), (3)(*a*), (4)(*b*).
(3)	1975 Sch. 6, para. 15(3)(*b*), (4)(*a*).
(4)	1975 Sch. 6, para. 15(3)(*bb*)(*bc*), (4) (*a*); 1976 s. 95(2).
(5)	1975 Sch. 6, para. 15(3)(*c*).

Clause of Bill	Derivation
(6)	1975 Sch. 6, para. 10(3), 15(5).
24(1)(2)	1975 Sch. 6, para. 11(1), (2).
(3)	1975 Sch. 6, para. 15(1), (2), (3), (4); 1976 s. 95(2).
24(4)	1975 Sch. 6, para. 15(5).
25(1)	1975 Sch. 6, para. 12.
(2)	1975 Sch. 6, para. 15(1), (2), (3), (4), (5); 1976 s. 95(2).
26(1)	1975 Sch. 6, para. 13(1).
(2)	1975 Sch. 6, para. 13(2); 1976 s. 85.
(3)	1975 Sch. 6, para. 13(3); 1976 s. 111(4).
(4)	1975 Sch. 6, para. 13(4); 1976 s. 111(4).
(5)(6)	1975 Sch. 6, para. 13(5), (6).
(7)	1975 Sch. 6, para. 15(1), (2), (3), (4), (5); 1976 s. 95(2).
(8)(9)	1975 Sch. 6, para. 13(7), (8).
27	1982 s. 95(1), (2).
28	1978 s. 67(1) to (6).
29(1)	1976 s. 117(1).
(2)	1976 s. 117(2), (6).
(3)(4)	1976 s. 117(3), (4).
(5)	1976 s. 117(5), (6); 1983 (No. 2) s. 9(2).
30	1976 s. 76(1) to (4).
31	1976 s. 77.
32	1976 s. 78.
33(1)	1976 s. 79(1); 1982 Sch. 17, para. 24(2).
(2)	1976 s. 82A(5)(*a*); 1982 Sch. 17, para. 26.
(3)(4)	1976 s. 79(3), (4).
(5)	1976 s. 82A(1), (2), (3); 1982 Sch. 17, para. 6.
(6)	1976 s. 82A(4); 1982 Sch. 17, para. 26.
(7)	1976 s. 79(7).
34(1)	1976 s. 80(1).
(2)	1976 s. 80(2); 1982 Sch. 17, para. 25(2), (3).
(3)	1976 s. 80(3); 1982 Sch. 17, para. 25(2), (3).
(4)	1976 s. 80(4).
35(1)	—
(2)	1976 s. 83(3).
(3)	1976 s. 83(4).
36	1975 Sch. 6, para. 16; 1976 s. 96(2), Sch. 11, para. 5; 1982 s. 95(3).
37	1975 Sch. 6, paras. 17, 18.
38(1)	1975 Sch. 6, para. 19(1); 1976 s. 96(3).
(2)	1975 Sch. 6, para. 19(2).
(3)	1975 Sch. 6, para. 19(3); 1976 s. 96(4).
(4)	1975 Sch. 6, para. 19(3A); 1976 s. 96(4).
(5)	1975 Sch. 6, para. 19(3B); 1976 s. 96(4).
(6)	1975 Sch. 6, para. 19(4).

Clause of Bill	Derivation
39	1975 Sch. 6, para. 20.
40	1975 Sch. 6, para. 21.
41	1975 Sch. 6, para. 22; 1976 s. 96(5).
42(1)(2)	1975 Sch. 6, para. 23(1), (2).
(3)	1975 Sch. 6, para. 23(3); 1976 s. 96(6).
(4)	1975 Sch. 6, para. 22A(1), (2), (4); 1976 s. 96(7).
43(1) to (3)	1975 Sch. 5, para. 1(1) to (3).
(4)	1975 Sch. 5, para. 1(4), (5); 1980 s. 93(2)(*a*).
(5)	1975 Sch. 5, para. 1(10).
44(1)	1975 Sch. 5, para. 1(1), (6).
(2)	1975 Sch. 5, para. 1(8); 1982 Sch. 17, para. 16; 1984 Sch. 21, para. 10.
45	1975 Sch. 5, para. 1(1), (7).
46	1975 Sch. 5, para. 1(9); 1976 Sch. 14, para. 10; 1980 s. 93 (2)(*b*).
47	1975 s. 51(1); 1980 s. 93(1).
48(1)	1975 s. 24(3); 1976 s. 120(1); 1981 s. 104(3).
(2)	1976 s. 120(2); 1981 s. 104(3).
(3)	1975 Sch. 5, para. 2(1).
(4)	1975 Sch. 7, para. 3(1), (2); 1982 Sch. 17, para. 19(2), (3).
(5)	1975 Sch. 7, para. 3(2A); 1978 s. 72; 1982 Sch. 17, para. 19(4).
(6)	1975 Sch. 7, para. 3(2AA); 1984 s. 101(2).
(7)	1975 Sch. 7, para. 3(4); 1982 Sch. 17, para 19(5).
49(1)	1975 Sch. 5, para. 3(1).
(2)	1978 s. 69(7).
50(1) to (3)	1975 Sch. 5, para. 3(2) to (4).
(4)	1975 Sch. 5, para. 3(4), (7).
(5)(6)	1975 Sch. 5, para. 3(5), (6).
51(1)	1975 Sch. 5, para. 4(1).
(2)	1975 s. 46(5).
(3)	1975 Sch. 5, para. 4(10); 1983 Sch. 9, para. 5.
52(1)	1975 Sch. 5, para. 4(2).
(2)	1975 Sch. 5, para. 4(4).
(3)(4)	1975 Sch. 5, para. 4(9), (10).
53(1)	1975 Sch. 5, para. 4(11).
(2)	1975 Sch. 5, para. 4(3).
(3)	1975 Sch. 5, para. 4(5).
(4)	1975 Sch. 5, para. 4(6); 1976 s. 110(2).
(5)	1975 Sch. 5, para. 4(5), (6); 1976 s. 110(2); 1978 s. 69(1); 1981 s. 104(1).
(6)	1978 s. 69(6).
(7)(8)	1978 s. 69(8).
54(1)	1975 s. 22(2).
(2)	1975 s. 22(3); 1976 s. 110(1).
(3)	1975 s. 22(2), (3); 1976 s. 110(1); 1978 s. 69(1), (6); 1981 s. 104(1).

Clause of Bill	Derivation
(4)	1975 s. 22(9).
55(1)	1975 s. 23(3).
(2)	1975 s. 20(4).
56(1)	1975 Sch. 6, para. 15(2A); 1981 s. 104(2); 1982 s. 95(2).
(2)	1975 Sch. 6, para. 15(4A); 1976 s. 95(3); 1978 s. 69(4).
(3)	1975 Sch. 6, para. 15(3)(*ba*), (4B); 1976 s. 95(2); 1978 s. 69(5); 1982 s. 95(2).
(4)	1975 Sch. 6, para. 15(4B); 1978 s. 69(5); 1982 s. 95(2).
(5)	1978 s. 69(6).
(6)	1976 s. 117(1), (6).
(7)	1976 s. 95(4); 1978 s. 69(8).
(8)	1978 s. 69(8).
57(1) to (4)	1981 s. 94(3) to (6).
(5)	1982 s. 95(1).
58(1)(2)	1982 s. 102(1)(2).
(3)	1982 s. 126(2).
59(1)(2)	1982 s. 103(1)(2).
(3)	1982 s. 103(3); 1982 c. 50 Sch. 5, para 28(*a*).
60	1982 s. 104.
61(1)	1976 ss. 82(11), 82A(7); 1982 s. 105(1), Sch. 17, para. 26.
(2) to (4)	1982 s. 105(2) to (4).
62	1982 s. 106.
63	1976 s. 82(6); 1982 s. 126(1), Sch. 17, para. 26.
64	1982 s. 107.
65	1982 s. 108.
66(1) to (4)	1982 s. 109(1) to (4).
(5)	1975 s. 20(5); 1982 s. 109(5).
(6)	1982 s. 110(7), Sch. 15, para. 2.
67(1)(2)	1982 s. 110(1)(2).
(3)	1975 s. 20(5); 1982 s. 110(3).
(4)	1975 s. 20(5); 1982 s. 110(3), Sch. 15, para. 3.
(5) to (7)	1982 s. 110(4) to (6).
68(1) to (3)	1982 s. 111(1) to (3).
(4)	1975 s. 20(5); 1982 s. 111(4).
(5)	1982 s. 111(5).
(6)	1982 Sch. 15, paras. 4(1), 5, 4 to 8.
69	1982 s. 112.
70(1) to (6)	1982 s. 113(1) to (6).
(7)	1982 s. 113(6A); 1984 s. 102(1).
(8)	1982 s. 113(7); 1984 s. 99(2).
(9)	1982 s. 113(8), Sch. 15, paras. 6 to 8.
(10)	1982 s. 113(9).
71(1) to (4)	1982 s. 114(1) to (4).
(5)	1982 s. 114(5); 1984 s. 102(1).
(6) to (8)	1982 s. 114(6) to (8).

Clause of Bill	Derivation
72(1) to (4)	1982 s. 116(1) to (4).
(5)	1982 s. 116(5); 1984 s. 102(1).
(6)	1982 s. 116(6).
73(1)	1982 s. 118(1)(*a*).
(2)	1982 s. 118(2), (4).
(3)	1982 s. 118(3); 1984 s. 102(1).
74(1)	1975 Sch. 5, para. 19(1) (pre-1981); 1981 s. 103; 1982 s. 118(1)(*b*).
(2)	1982 s. 118(2), (4).
(3)	1982 s. 118(3); 1984 s. 102(1).
(4)	1975 Sch. 5, para. 19(4) (pre-1981); 1977 s. 51(5); 1983 c. 20 Sch. 4, para. 40.
75	1982 s. 115.
76(1)	1982 s. 119(1).
76(2)	1975 Sch. 6, para. 13(7); 1976 s. 111(4); 1982 s. 119(2).
(3) to (8)	1982 s. 119(3) to (8).
77	—
78(1)(2)	1976 s. 81(1), (2); 1982 Sch. 17, para. 26.
(3)	1976 ss. 81(3), 82A(1) to (4), 83(3A); 1982 Sch. 17, paras. 26, 27.
(4)	1976 s. 82A(5), (7); 1982 Sch. 17, para. 26.
(5)	1976 s. 82A(6); 1982 Sch. 17, para. 26.
(6)	1976 s. 81(4); 1982 Sch. 17, para. 26.
79(1) to (7)	1976 s. 82(1) to (7); 1982 Sch. 17, para. 26.
(8)(9)	1976 s. 82(9), (10); 1982 Sch. 17, para. 26.
(10)	1976 s. 83(4).
80(1)	1982 s. 120(1); 1984 Sch. 21, para 23.
(2)(3)	1982 s. 120(2)(3).
81	1982 s. 121; 1984 s. 101(1), Sch. 21, para. 23.
82(1)	1982 s. 122(1); 1984 Sch. 21, para. 24.
(2)(3)	1982 s. 122(2)(3).
83	1982 s. 123; 1984 Sch. 21, para. 23.
84	1982 s. 124; 1984 Sch. 21, para. 24.
85	1982 s. 125.
86(1)	1975 Sch. 5, para. 17(1); 1982 s. 98(2).
(2)	1975 Sch. 5, para. 17(1A); 1982 s. 98(4).
(3)	1975 Sch. 5, para. 17(2); 1982 s. 98(5).
(4)	1975 Sch. 5, para. 17(3); 1984 Sch. 21, para. 12.
(5)	1975 Sch. 5, para. 17(4A); 1976 s. 107(2).
87(1)	1975 Sch. 5, para. 17A(1); 1976 s. 108(1); 1982 s. 98(6).
(2)(3)	1975 Sch. 5, para. 17A(2)(3); 1976 s. 108(1).
88(1)	1975 Sch. 5, para. 18(1); 1978 s. 71(2).
(2)	1975 Sch. 5, para. 18(2); 1978 s. 71(1).
89(1) to (3)	1975 Sch. 5, para. 19(1) to (3); 1981 s. 103.
(4)	1975 Sch. 5, para. 19(4); 1981 s. 103; 1983 c. 20 Sch. 4, para. 40.

Clause of Bill	Derivation
90	1975 Sch. 5, para. 19A; 1976 s. 109.
91(1)	1975 Sch. 5, para. 22(1); 1984 Sch. 21, para. 13.
(2)	1975 Sch. 5, para. 22(2).
92	1975 Sch. 5, para. 22A(1)(2); 1976 s. 105(1).
93	1975 s. 47(4).
94(1)	1975 s. 39(1), (9).
(2)	1975 s. 39(2); 1976 s. 118(6).
(3)	1975 s. 39(6A); 1976 s. 118(1).
(4)	1975 s. 39(4)
(5)	1975 Sch. 6, para. 8; 1976 s. 118(8).
95	1975 s. 39(8D); 1976 s. 118(1).
96	1975 s. 39(8A); 1976 s. 118(1).
97	1975 s. 39(8B), (8C); 1976 s. 118(1).
98(1)	1975 s. 39(5); 1976 s. 118(7).
(2)	1975 s. 39(6).
99(1)	1975 Sch. 5, para. 24(1); 1976 s. 118(5); 1984 Sch. 21, para. 14(2).
(2)	1975 Sch. 5, para. 24(2); 1982 s. 99(2).
(3)	1975 Sch. 5, para. 24(3).
100	1976 s. 118(2)(3).
101(1)	1975 Sch. 5, para. 24(5); 1982 s. 99(3); 1984 Sch. 21, para. 14(3).
(2)	1975 Sch. 5, para. 24(5A); 1982 s. 99(4).
102(1)	1975 s. 39(6), Sch.5, para. 24(6); 1982 s. 99(5).
(2)	1975 s. 39(8).
103(1)	1976 Sch. 10, para. 1; 1982 Sch. 17, para. 30.
(2)	1976 Sch. 10, para. 13(1).
(3)	1976 Sch. 10, para. 3(1).
104(1)	1976 Sch. 10, para. 2(1), (1A); 1978 s. 64(2); 1981 s. 100(2); 1983 (No. 2) s. 10(1).
(2)	1976 Sch. 10, para. 2(2).
105(1)	1976 Sch. 10, para. 3(1); 1978 s. 64(3); 1981 s. 100(3).
(2)	1976 Sch. 10, para. 3(1A); 1978 s. 64(4).
(3)(4)	1976 Sch. 10, para. 3(2), (3).
(5)	1976 Sch. 10, para. 3(5).
(6)	1976 Sch. 10, para. 3(6); 1981 s. 100(4).
106	1976 Sch. 10, para. 4(1).
107(1)	1976 Sch. 10, para. 4(1).
(2)(3)	1976 Sch. 10, para. 4(2), (3).
(4)	1976 Sch. 10, para. 4(5); 1978 s. 64(5); 1979 c. 14 Sch. 7, para. 9.
108	1976 Sch. 10, para. 4(4).
109	1976 Sch. 10, para. 5.

Clause of Bill	Derivation
110	1976 Sch. 10, para. 6.
111	1976 Sch. 10, para. 7.
112	1976 Sch. 10, para. 8.
113	1976 Sch. 10, para. 3(4).
114(1)	1976 Sch. 10, para. 10; 1981 s. 96(3)(*d*).
(2)	1976 Sch. 10, para. 11.
115(1)	1981 Sch. 14, para. 1(1); 1982 Sch. 17, para. 34.
(2) to (4)	1981 Sch. 14, para. 1(2) to (4).
116(1)	1981 Sch. 14, para. 2(1).
(2)	1981 Sch. 14, para. 2(2); 1983 (No. 2) s. 10(2).
(3)	1981 Sch. 14, para. 2(3).
(4)	1981 Sch. 14, para. 2(4); 1983 (No. 2) s. 10(2).
(5) to (7)	1981 Sch. 14, para. 2(5) to (7).
117	1981 Sch. 14, para. 3.
118	1981 Sch. 14, para. 4.
119	1981 Sch. 14, para. 5.
120(1)	1981 Sch. 14, para. 7.
(2)	1981 Sch. 14, para. 6.
121	1981 Sch. 14, para. 8.
122(1)(2)	1981 Sch. 14, para. 9.
(3)	1981 Sch. 14, para. 10.
123(1)	1981 Sch. 14, para. 11.
(2) to (4)	1981 Sch. 14, para. 12.
(5)	1981 Sch. 14, para. 13.
124	1981 Sch. 14, para. 14.
125(1)	1975 Sch. 9, paras. 1(1), 5(1); 1981 s. 96(3)(*a*).
(2)	1975 Sch. 9, para. 1(1).
(3)	1975 Sch. 9, para. 1(2).
126(1)	1975 Sch. 9, para. 2(1).
(2)(3)	1975 Sch. 9, para. 2(3), (4).
127(1)	1975 Sch. 9, para. 3(1).
(2)	1975 Sch. 9, para. 3(2); 1978 s. 65(1).
128	1975 Sch. 9, para. 3(1).
129	1975 Sch. 9, para. 4.
130(1)	1975 Sch. 9, para. 6(1).
(2)	1975 Sch. 9, para. 6(2); 1976 s. 75.
131(1)	1976 s. 99(1).
(2)	1976 s. 99(2), (3).
(3)	1976 s. 99(6).

Clause of Bill	Derivation
132(1)	1976 s. 99(4).
(2)	1976 s. 99(7).
133	1976 Sch. 12, para. 2.
134	1976 Sch. 12, para. 3.
135(1)(2)	1976 Sch. 12, para. 4(1), (2); 1979 c. 14 Sch. 7, para. 9.
(3) to (5)	1976 Sch. 12, para. 4(3) to (5).
136	1976 Sch. 12, para. 5.
137	1976 Sch. 12, para. 6.
138(1)	1976 Sch. 12, para. 7(1).
(2)	1976 Sch. 12, para. 7(2); 1979 c. 14 Sch. 7, para. 9.
139(1) to (3)	1976 Sch. 12, para. 8.
(4)	1976 Sch. 12, para. 9.
140(1)	1976 Sch. 12, para. 1.
(2)	1976 s. 99(5).
141	1981 s. 101(1) to (7).
142(1) to (4)	1978 s. 68(1) to (4).
(5)(6)	1978 s. 68(5).
(7)	1978 s. 68(4); 1980 s. 93(3).
143	1975 s. 47(1B); 1975 s. 121(1).
144	1975 s. 47(1A)(1AA); 1976 s. 121(1); 1982 Sch. 17, para. 4; 1984 s. 100.
145	1975 s. 47(3).
146(1) to (5)	1976 s. 122(1) to (5).
(6)	1975 s. 122(6); 1982 Sch. 17, para. 29.
(7)	1976 s. 122(7).
(8)	1976 s. 122(7A); 1980 s. 92.
(9)	1976 s. 122(8A); S.I. 1979/927.
147(1) to (4)	1976 s. 123(1) to (4).
(5) to (9)	1976 s. 123(7) to (11).
148(1)	1976 s. 86(1); 1981 s. 93(2).
(2) to (4)	1976 s. 86(2) to (4).
(5)	1976 s. 86(6); 1980 s. 87(2); 1981 s. 96(3)(*b*).
149(1)	1976 s. 87(1); 1981 s. 93(3).
(2) to (4)	1976 s. 87(2) to (4).
(5)	1976 s. 87(5); 1980 s. 87(3).
(6)	1976 s. 87(5A); 1980 s. 87(4); 1981 s. 96(3)(*c*).
(7)	1976 s. 87(6).
(8)(9)	1976 s. 87(8), (9).
150	1976 s. 88(1), (2).
151(1)	1975 Sch. 5, para. 16(1); 1976 Sch. 14, para.18.
(2) to (4)	1975 Sch. 5, para. 16(2) to (4).

Clause of Bill	Derivation
(5)	1975 Sch. 5, para. 16(6); 1982 Sch. 17, para.17.
152	1975 Sch. 7, para. 2.
153(1)	1975 Sch. 7, para. 4(1).
(2)	1975 Sch. 7, para. 4(2); 1984 Sch. 21, para. 15.
(3)(4)	1975 Sch. 7, para. 4(3), (4).
154(1)(2)	1975 Sch. 7, para. 1(1), (2).
(3)	1981 c. 55 Sch. 5, saving.
155(1)	1975 Sch. 7, para. 6(1), (2); 1981 c. 61 s. 51(3).
(2) to (6)	1975 Sch. 7, para. 6(3) to (7).
(7)	1975 Sch. 7, para. 6(9).
156	1981 s. 135; 1982 s. 100.
157	1982 s. 96(1) to (5).
159	1975 Sch. 7, para. 7.
159	1975 Sch. 7, para. 8; 1976 s. 125.
160	1975 s. 38(1).
161(1)	1975 Sch. 10, para. 7(1).
(2)	1975 Sch. 10, para. 7(2); 1976 s. 103(1).
(3) to (5)	1975 Sch. 10, para. 7(3) to (5).
162(1)	1975 Sch. 10, para. 1(5).
(2)	1975 Sch. 10, para. 1(4).
(3)	1975 Sch. 10, para. 1(2).
(4)	1975 Sch. 10, para. 2.
(5)	1975 Sch. 10, para. 3.
163(1)	1975 Sch. 10, para. 5(1); 1984 Sch. 21, para. 17.
(2)(3)	1975 Sch. 10, para. 5(2), (3).
164	1975 s. 51(1); Sch. 10, para. 6.
165(1)	1975 Sch. 10, para. 4(1); 1979 c. 14 Sch. 7, paras. 8, 9.
(2)	1975 Sch. 10, para. 4(2); 1982 Sch. 17, para. 20.
166	1975 Sch. 10, para. 10.
167(1)	1975 Sch. 10, para. 11(1)
(2)	1975 Sch. 10, para. 11(2); 1976 ss. 86(7), 87(5B); 1978 s. 73(1); 1980 s. 87(2), (4).
(3)(4)	1975 Sch. 10, para. 11(3)(4).
(5)	1975 Sch. 10, para. 11(5); 1982 Sch. 17, para. 22.
168	1975 Sch. 10, para. 13.
169	1975 Sch. 10, para. 12.
170	1975 Sch. 10, para. 8.
171(1)	1975 Sch. 10, para. 9(1)(*a*).
(2)	1975 Sch. 10, para. 9(2); 176 s. 118(9).
172	1975 Sch. 10, para. 9(1)(*b*).

Clause of Bill	Derivation
173	1975 Sch. 10, para. 9(1)(*d*).
174(1)	1975 Sch. 10, para. 9(1)(*e*)(*f*); 1984 s. 93(8), Sch. 9, para. 13.
(2)	1975 s. 51(1), Sch. 10, para. 9(2A); 1976 s. 100(1).
175	1975 Sch. 10, para. 9(1)(*c*).
176	1975 Sch. 10, para. 9A; 1976 s. 102(1); 1982 Sch. 17, para.21.
177(1)	1981 s. 98(1).
(2)	1982 s. 97(1).
(3)	1981 s. 98(1); 1982 s. 97(1).
(4)	1982 s. 97(2).
178(1)	1975 s. 51(1), Sch.19, para. 14(1).
(2)	1976 s. 104.
(3)	1975 Sch. 10, para. 14(2).
(4)	1975 Sch. 10, para. 19.
(5)	1975 Sch. 10, para. 21.
179(1)	1975 Sch. 10, para. 15.
(2)	1975 Sch. 10, para. 16.
(3)	1975 Sch. 10, para. 20.
180(1)	1975 Sch. 10, para. 17.
(2)(3)	1975 Sch. 10, para. 18(1), (2).
181	1975 Sch. 10, para. 25.
182	1975 Sch. 10, para. 26.
183(1)(2)	1975 Sch. 10, para. 27(1), (2); 1979 c. 14 Sch.7, para. 9.
(3) to (6)	1975 Sch. 10, para. 27(3) to (6).
184	1975 Sch. 10, para. 24.
185(1)(2)	1975 Sch. 10, para. 28(1), (2).
(3)	1975 Sch. 10, para. 18(2).
186	1975 Sch. 10, para. 23.
187(1)	1975 Sch. 10, para. 29(1); 1979 c. 14 Sch. 7, para. 8.
(2) to (6)	1975 Sch. 10, para. 29(2) to (6).
188	1975 Sch. 10, para. 30.
189	1975 Sch. 10, para. 22.
190(1)	1975 s. 51(1), Sch. 10, para. 31(1); 1976 s. 101(2), Sch. 13.
(2)	1975 Sch. 10, para. 32(4); 1976 s. 101(2), Sch. 13.
(3)	1975 Sch. 10, para. 31(2); 1976 s. 101(2), Sch. 13.
(4)	1975 Sch. 10, para. 39; 1976 s. 101(2), Sch. 13.
191	1975 Sch. 10, para. 32(1) to (3); 1976 s. 101(2), Sch. 13.
192	1975 Sch. 10, para. 37; 1976 s. 101(2), Sch.13.
193	1975 Sch. 10, para. 33; 1976 s. 101(2), Sch. 13.
194(1)	1975 Sch. 10, para. 34(1); 1976 s. 101(2), Sch. 13.
(2)	1975 Sch. 10, para. 34(2); 1976 s. 101(2), Sch. 13; c. 14 Sch. 7, para. 9.

Clause of Bill	Derivation
195	1975 Sch. 10, para. 35; 1976 s. 101(2), Sch. 13.
196	1975 Sch. 10, para. 36; 1976 s. 101(2), Sch. 13.
197	1975 Sch. 10, para. 38; 1976 s. 101(2), Sch. 13.
198(1) to (3)	1975 Sch. 10, para. 40(1) to (3); 1976 s. 101(2), Sch. 13.
(4)	1975 Sch. 10, para. 40(4); 1976 s. 101(2), Sch. 13; 1981 c. 66 Sch. 3, para. 2.
199(1)	1975 s. 25(2), (9).
(2)	1975 s. 25(4).
(3)	1975 s. 26(1).
(4)	1975 s. 25(6).
(5)	1975 s. 25(10).
200(1)	1975 s. 25(5).
(2)	1975 s. 26(1).
(3)	1975 s. 25(5).
(4)	1975 s. 25(6), (10).
201(1)	1975 s. 25(3); 1982 Sch. 17, para. 1.
(2)	1975 s. 25(4).
(3)	1976 Sch. 14, para. 20.
(4)	1975 Sch. 5, para. 1(8).
(5)	1975 s. 25(9), 1982 Sch. 17, para. 2.
(6)	1975 s. 25(10).
202(1)	1975 s. 39(3), Sch. 5, para. 24(1); 1984 Sch. 21, para. 14 (2).
(2)	1975 s. 39(3)(*a*), (*b*).
(3)	1975 s. 39(3)(*c*).
(4)	1975 s. 26(2); 1984 Sch. 21 para. 3(*b*).
203(1)	1975 s. 25(8); 1976 s. 119(1).
(2) to (4)	1974 s. 119(2) to (4).
204(1) to (4)	1975 s. 27(1) to (4).
(5)	1975 s. 27(5); 1981 s. 46(8).
(6)(7)	1975 s. 27(6), (7).
205	1975 s. 25(1).
206	1975 s. 26(3).
207(1)	1976 s. 78(2), (3).
(2)	1976 s. 78(3); 1977 s. 53.
(3)	1976 s. 82(8); 1982 Sch. 17, para. 26.
(4)	1975 ss. 32(1), 34(3).
(5)	1975 ss. 32(2); 1977 s. 53.
208	1975 Sch. 9, para. 2(2).
209(1)	1975 s. 26(4).
(2)(3)	1976 s. 123(5).
210	1975 sch, 5, para. 16(3).
211(1)(2)	1975 s. 28(1); 1983 (No. 2) s. 13(1).
(3)	1975 s. 28(1A); 1983 (No. 2) s. 13(1).
(4)	1975 s. 28(8); 1983 (No. 2) s. 13(2).

Clause of Bill	Derivation
212(1) to (3)	1975 s. 28(3) to (5).
(4)	1975 s. 28(8); 1983 (No. 2) s. 13(2).
213	1975 s. 28(2).
214(1)(2)	1975 s. 28(6), (7).
(3)	1975 s. 28(8); 1983 (No. 2) s. 13(2).
215	1975 Sch. 4, para. 1.
216(1)	1975 Sch. 4, para. 2(1); 1976 Sch. 14, para. 4; 1982 Sch. 17, para 7.
(2)	1975 Sch. 4, para. 2(2A); 1980 s. 94(4); 1983 Sch. 9, para. 4.
(3)(4)	1975 Sch. 4, para. 2(2), (3); 1982 Sch. 17, para. 7.
(5)	1975 Sch. 4, para. 2(4); 1980 s. 94(5).
(6)	1975 Sch. 4, para. 2(5); 1980 s. 94(6).
(7)	1975 Sch. 4, para. 2(7); 1976 Sch. 11, para. 3; 1982 Sch. 17, para. 7.
217	1975 Sch. 4, para. 3.
218(1)(2)	1975 Sch. 4, para. 4(1), (2).
(3)	1975 Sch. 4, para. 4(3); 1982 Sch. 17, para. 8.
219	1975 Sch. 4, para. 5.
220(1)	1975 Sch. 4, para. 11(1).
(2)	1975 Sch. 4, para. 11(2); 1975 c. 21 ss. 289F(1), (8), 289G(1) to (5); 1982 c. 48 ss. 37, 38(1), (6), (8), 46(1), (4)(*a*), 54.
221(1) to (5)	1975 Sch. 4, para. 6(1) to (5).
(6)	1975 Sch. 4, para. 6(6); 1976 Sch. 14, para. 5; 1984 Sch. 21, para. 6.
222	1975 Sch. 4, para. 7.
223	1975 Sch. 4, para. 8.
224	1975 Sch. 4, para. 9.
225(1)	1975 Sch. 4, para. 10(1).
(2)	1975 Sch. 4, para. 10(2); 1984 Sch. 22, para. 6.
(3)(6)	1975 Sch. 4, para. 10(3) to (6).
(7)	1984 s. 122(2).
226(1) to (3)	1975 Sch. 4, para. 12(1) to (3).
(4)	1975 Sch. 4, para. 12(4); 1976 Sch. 11, para. 3; 1982 Sch. 17, para. 10.
(5)(6)	1975 Sch. 4, para. 12(5), (6).
227(1)	1975 Sch. 4, paras. 13(1), (5), 14(1), (4); 1982 Sch. 17, paras. 11, 12; 1983 (No. 2) s. 11(1).
(2)	1975 Sch. 4, paras. 13(1), 14(1).
(3)	1975 Sch. 4, paras. 13(1), (6), 14(1), (5).
(4)	1975 Sch. 4, paras. 13(4), 14(3).
(5)	1975 Sch. 4, paras. 13(6), 14(5).
(6)	1975 Sch. 4, para. 14(3).
(7)	1975 Sch. 4, para. 14(1), (2), (6); 1984 Sch. 21, para. 7.
228(1)	1975 Sch. 4, para. 13(1), (6); 1982 Sch. 17, para. 11.

Clause of Bill	Derivation
(2)	1975 Sch. 4, para. 13(2).
(3)	1975 Sch. 4, para. 13(3), (6); 1983 (No. 2) s. 11(2).
(4)	1975 Sch. 4, para. 13(8).
229	1975 Sch. 4, para 15; 1983 (No. 2) s. 11(1).
230(1)	1975 Sch. 4, paras. 17(1), 19(6); 1980 c. 17 ss. 12(1)(*a*), 13(1); S.I. 1983/879 Sch. 2, para. 1(2).
(2)	1975 Sch. 4, para. 17(2).
(3)	1975 Sch. 4, para. 17(3); 1979 c. 46 Sch. 4, para. 15; 1980 c. 17 s. 12(1)(*b*); S.I. 1983/879 Sch. 2, para. 1(3); S.R. (N.I.) 1976/80.
(4)	1975 Sch. 4, para. 17(4); 1976 s. 124; 1980 c. 17 s. 12(1)(*b*); S.I. 1983/879 Sch. 2, para. 1(4).
(5)	1975 Sch. 4, para. 17(5); 1980 c. 17 s. 12(1)(*d*); S.I. 1983/879 Sch. 2, para. 1(5).
231(1)	1975 Sch. 4, para. 18(1).
(2)	1975 Sch. 4, para. 19(6); 1980 c. 17 s. 13(1).
(3)	1975 Sch. 4, para. 18(2).
232	1975 Sch. 4, para. 27.
233(1)	1975 Sch. 4, para. 19(1); 1976 s. 83(5), Sch. 11, para. 3; 1982 Sch. 17, para. 13.
(2)	1975 Sch. 4, para. 19(1); S.I. 1982/1585.
(3)(4)	1975 Sch. 4, para. 19(4), (5).
234(1)(2)	1975 Sch. 4, para. 16(1), (2); 1981 s. 96(2).
(3)	1975 Sch. 4, para. 16(3).
235	1975 Sch. 4, para. 19(3), (4).
236(1)	1975 Sch. 4, para. 19(2).
(2)	1976 s. 122(8), (8A); S.I. 1979/927.
(3)	1976 ss. 87(7), 88(3), 122(8).
(4)	1976 s. 123(2), (4); 1984 Sch. 21, para. 20.
237(1)	1975 Sch. 4, para. 20(1); 1982 Sch. 17, para. 14.
(2) to (6)	1975 Sch. 4, para. 20(2) to (6).
238(1)	1975 Sch. 4, para. 21(1), (4).
(2)(3)	1975 Sch. 4, para. 21(2), (3).
239(1) to (3)	1975 Sch. 4, para. 25(1) to (3).
(4)	1975 Sch. 4, para. 25(4); 1978 s. 68(6).
(5)	1975 Sch. 4, para. 25(5); 1976 Sch. 14, para. 7; 1982 Sch. 17, para. 15.
240(1)(2)	1975 Sch. 4, para. 23(1), (2).
(3)	1975 Sch. 4, para. 23(3); 1984 s. 102(1).
241	1975 Sch. 4, para. 24.
242	1975 Sch. 4, para. 22.
243	1975 Sch. 4, para. 22A; 1984 s. 103(1).
244	1975 Sch. 4, para. 22B; 1984 s. 103(1).
245	1975 Sch. 4, para. 28.

Clause of Bill	Derivation
246	1975 Sch. 4, para. 29.
247	1975 Sch. 4, para. 30.
248	1975 Sch. 4, para. 31.
249	1975 Sch. 4, para. 32.
250	1975 Sch. 4, para. 33.
251	1975 Sch. 4, para. 35.
252	1975 Sch. 4, para. 34.
253	1975 Sch. 4, para. 37.
254(1)	1975 Sch. 4, para. 36.
(2)	1975 Sch. 4, para. 36A; 1984 s. 103(2).
255	1975 Sch. 4, para. 26.
256(1)	1980 s. 94(1).
(2)	1980 s. 94(2); 1981 c. 54 Sch. 5.
(3)	1980 s. 94(3).
(4)	1980 s. 94(9).
257(1)(2)	1975 Sch. 4, para. 39(1), (2).
(3)	1975 Sch. 4, para. 39(3); S.I. 1979/1575 Sch. 2, para. 12.
258	1975 Sch. 4, para. 41.
259	1975 Sch. 4, para. 42(2).
260	1975 Sch. 4, para. 42(1).
261	1975 Sch. 4, para. 40.
262	1975 s. 40.
263	1975 s. 42.
264(1)	1976 s. 114(1).
(2)(3)	1976 s. 114(2), (3); 1981 s. 93(4).
(4)(5)	1976 s. 114(3A), (3B); 1981 s. 93(4).
(6)(7)	1976 s. 114(4), (5).
(8)	1976 s. 114(6); 1981 s. 93(5); 1983 Sch. 9, para. 7.
(9)	1976 s. 114(7).
265	1975 s. 43(1).
266(1)	1975 s. 43(2).
(2)(3)	1975 s. 43(3), (4); 1976 s. 113(1).
(4)	1975 s. 43(5); 1976 s. 113(1); 1982 Sch. 17, para. 3.
267(1)	1975 s. 45(1); 1984 Sch. 21, para. 4.
(2)	1975 Sch. 7, paras. 3(3), 5(2), 7(6).
(3)	1975 s. 45(1), Sch. 5, para. 2(2); 1982 ss. 108(8), 122(4).
(4)	1975 s. 45(2).
268	1975 s. 44.

Clause of Bill	Derivation
269(1) to (3)	1975 Sch. 4, para. 13(7); 1976 Sch. 10, para. 13(2); 1981 Sch. 14, para. 15.
(4)	1975 Sch. 4, para. 13(7); 1976 Sch. 10, para. 13(2); 1978 s. 66(1), (2); 1981 Sch. 14, para. 15.
270	1975 s. 51(4); 1979 c. 14 Sch. 7, paras 8(*a*), 9.
271	1975 s. 51(5); 1982 Sch. 17, para. 6.
272	1975 s. 51(1); 1984 Sch. 21, para. 5(*b*) (" land "); 1975 s. 59(2) (" the Taxes Act ").
273 to 278	—
Sch. 1	1975 s. 37(3); 1984 s. 98.
Sch. 2	
para. 1	1980 Sch. 15, para. 1.
2	1980 Sch. 15, para. 2.
3	1980 Sch. 15, para. 2A; 1982 Sch. 17, para. 31; 1984 Sch. 21, para. 21.
4	1980 Sch. 15, para. 4.
5	1980 Sch. 15, para. 5; 1984 Sch. 21, para. 21.
6	1980 Sch. 15, para. 6; 1982 Sch. 17, para. 32; 1984 Sch. 21, para. 21.
7	1980 Sch. 15, para. 7.
Sch. 3	1975 Sch. 6, para. 12; 1980 s. 118(5); 1983 s. 46(5).
Sch. 4	
para. 1(1)	1982 s. 93(1).
(2)	1982 s. 93(9).
(3)	1982 s. 94(5).
2(1)	1982 s. 93(2).
(2)(3)	1982 s. 94(1).
3(1)	1982 s. 93(3).
(2) to (4)	1982 s. 94(2) to (4).
(5)	1982 s. 94(6).
4	1982 s. 93(4), (5).
5 to 7	1982 s. 93(6) to (8).
8 to 15	1982 Sch. 16, paras. 2 to 9.
16 to 18	1982 Sch. 16, para. 1.
Sch. 5	
para. 1	1975 s. 32.
2(1)	1975 s. 33(1).
(2)	1975 s. 33(3); 1976 s. 83(2).
(3), (4)	1975 s. 33(4), (5).
3(1) to (4)	1975 s. 34(3) to (6).
(5)	1975 s. 34(9).
4	1975 s. 34(8); 1976 s. 83(2).
5(1)	1975 s. 31(2).
(2)	1975 s. 34(2).
(3)	1975 s. 31(3).
6	1976 s. 83(2).
Sch. 6	
para. 1	1975 s. 49(5), Sch. 12, para. 1.
2	1975 s. 22(4), Sch. 5, para. 4(7); 1984 Sch. 5, paras. 1, 11.

Clause of Bill	Derivation
3	1975 Sch. 5, para. 23.
4(1)	1976 s. 83(6).
(2)	1976 s. 83(3A), (7); 1982 Sch. 17, para. 27.
(3)	1976 s. 83(7).
(4)(5)	1976 s. 83(8), (9).

PART 1: TEXT

Introduction (pp 1-8)

The £55,000 threshold mentioned on p **1** was raised to £60,000 by the Finance (No 2) Act 1983 with effect from 15 March 1983 and to £64,000 by the Finance Act 1984 with effect from 13 March 1984. In the 1984 scale of rates the top rate on death (or within three years before death) is 60 per cent, and the lifetime rates are exactly half the death rates in all bands.

The Finance (No 2) Act 1983 made the following further changes, all with effect from 15 March 1983:

(1) the limit of £250,000 for the charity exemption (p **2**) is abolished;

(2) the 20 per cent agricultural relief and the 20 per cent business relief (p **4**) are increased to 30 per cent;

(3) persons who have acquired a domicile in the Channel Islands or the Isle of Man (p **5**) are no longer treated as retaining their United Kingdom domicile indefinitely;

(4) the eight-year period for instalments (p **6**) is increased to ten years.

In addition, the rates of interest on unpaid tax and on repayments, which were previously 9 per cent for transfers on death and 12 per cent for other transfers (p **6**), have been reduced by SI 1982 No 1585 to 6 per cent and 8 per cent respectively with effect from 1 December 1982.

Interpretation and Construction of the Taxing Acts (pp 10-44)

STRICT CONSTRUCTION

Lord Reid's observations in *Luke* v *IRC* [1963] AC 557, cited at p **14**, were relied on by the Revenue in *IRC* v *Trustees of Sir John Aird's Settlement (No 1)* [1983] STC 700 as establishing a general principle of construction. The Court of Appeal did not object to that but could not accept that para 6(7) of Sched 5 to the Finance Act 1975 showed an 'obvious intention' on the part of the legislature. Oliver LJ referred to *Lumsden* v *IRC* [1914] AC 877 (mentioned at p **17**), where Viscount Haldane said at p 892:

> 'But a mere conjecture that Parliament entertained a purpose which, however natural, has not been embodied in

the words it has used if they be literally interpreted is no sufficient reason for departing from the literal interpretation.'

Oliver LJ also quoted Lord Reid's remarks in *Stenhouse Holdings Ltd* v *IRC* (1970), 46 TC at p 682 (cited at p **17**) as indicating a broader approach to construction than was previously regarded as permissible, and said:

'Nevertheless there are limits within which it is permissible to reframe the express words which the legislature has chosen to use. Where it is clear that a literal reading produces a wholly unreasonable or administratively impossible result and there is a context for adopting a more restricted reading, there is no particular difficulty. *Camille Dreyfus* v *IRC* [1956] AC 39 and *IRC* v *Plummer* [1980] AC 896 were both cases in which a more limited construction was deducible from other provisions of the statute which pointed to the legislature's intention. Nor is there any particular difficulty where (as, for instance, in *R* v *Federal Steam Navigation Co* [1947] 1 WLR 505) it is impossible, on a literal construction, to give any intelligible meaning at all to the particular provision. But this case does not fall under either of these heads. Construed literally the paragraph is perfectly intelligible and perfectly capable of operation. The problem is simply that the consequences go a great deal further than the legislature can rationally have been supposed to have foreseen. That, no doubt, points to a more limited meaning having been intended, but one must, I think, start from the position that the intention has to be deduced from the words which Parliament has chosen to use and that they must be fairly capable of the more limited construction sought to be put upon them. If not, they must be applied as they stand, however strongly it may be suspected that this was not the real intention of Parliament.'

Jones v *Wroxham Park Estates Ltd* [1980] AC 74 was another case in which the literal interpretation of the words used produced consequences which could hardly have been foreseen. Lord Diplock at p 105 said:

'I am not reluctant to adopt a purposive construction where to apply the literal meaning of the legislative language used would lead to results which clearly defeat the purpose of the Act. But in doing so the task on which a court of justice is engaged remains one of construction, even where this involves reading into the Act words which are not expressly included in it. *Kammins Ballrooms Co Ltd* v *Zenith Investments (Torquay) Ltd*

[1971] AC 850 provides an instance of this; but in that case the three conditions that must be fulfilled in order to justify this course were satisfied.

(1) First, it was possible to determine from a consideration of the provisions of the Act read as a whole precisely what the mischief was that it was the purpose of the Act to remedy;
(2) secondly, it was apparent that the draftsman and Parliament had by inadvertence overlooked, and so omitted to deal with, an eventuality required to be dealt with if the purpose of the Act was to be achieved; and
(3) thirdly, it was possible to state with certainty what were the additional words that would have been inserted by the draftsman and approved by Parliament had their attention been drawn to the omission before the Bill passed into law.

Unless this third condition is fulfilled, any attempt by a court of justice to repair the omission in the Act cannot be justified as an exercise of its jurisdiction to determine what is the meaning of a written law which Parliament has passed. Such an attempt crosses the boundary between construction and legislation.'

In the *Aird (No 1)* case, cited above, Oliver LJ said that neither the first nor the third of the conditions stated by Lord Diplock could be said with confidence to be satisfied, and he was unable to find any justification as a matter of construction for departing from the literal meaning of the words. For further details of the judgment, *see* p 52–54, below.

PUNCTUATION

The relevance of punctuation, side-notes and cross-headings in statutes (pp **18–19**) was considered also in *R* v *Schildkamp* [1971] AC 1, where Lord Reid said at p 10:

'. . . it may be more realistic to accept the Act as printed as being the product of the whole legislative process, and to give due weight to everything found in the printed Act . . . I would not object to taking all these matters into account, provided that we realise that they cannot have equal weight with the words of the Act. Punctuation can be of some assistance in construction.'

In the same case Lord Upjohn said at p 28:

'When the court construing the statute is reading it through to

> understand it, it must read the cross-headings as well as the body of the statute, and that will always be a useful pointer as to the intention of Parliament in enacting the immediately following sections . . . A side-note is a very brief precis of the section and therefore forms a most unsure guide to the construction of the enacting section, but it is as much a part of the Bill as a cross-heading and I can conceive of cases where very rarely it might throw some light on the intentions of Parliament just as a punctuation mark.'

In *Hanlon* v *The Law Society* [1981] AC 124, Lord Lowry said at p 198:

> 'I consider that not to take account of punctuation disregards the reality that literate people, such as Parliamentary draftsmen, punctuate what they write, if not identically, at least in accordance with grammatical principles. Why should not other literate people, such as judges, look at the punctuation in order to interpret the meaning of the legislation as accepted by Parliament?'

R v *Governor of Brixton Prison, ex parte Naranjan Singh* [1962] 1 QB 211 and *Luby* v *Newcastle-under-Lyme Corporation* [1965] 1 QB 214 are sometimes cited as examples of the irrelevance of punctuation even in modern statutes. In the first case the court construed a statute as if a comma were inserted; in the other the Court of Appeal treated a comma as if it were not there. But that does not mean that they disregarded the punctuation. They looked at it and decided that the intention of the legislature, as manifested by the words used, must prevail over the punctuation.

In *Marshall* v *Cottingham* [1982] Ch 82 Megarry V-C said: 'I accept, of course, that the day is long past when the courts would pay no heed to punctuation in an Act of Parliament.'

The latest case on the subject appears to be *Egerton* v *IRC* [1983] STC 531, noted at p 57, below. The point to which the Court of Appeal attached most importance was that the last part of s 71(2) of the Finance Act 1978 was separated from the first part only by a semi-colon. In the first part Parliament had made clear its intention that the section as a whole was to be construed and applied on the footing that it came into force on 11 April 1978. Correspondingly, in the judgment of the Court, it had made clear its intention that the wording of the last part of the subsection should be read and applied on the same footing.

It appears that brackets, like other punctuation marks, are disregarded in statutes before 1850: *Devonshire (Duke of)* v *O'Connor*

(1890) 24 QBD 468, *per* Lord Esher MR at p 478; *R* v *Speyer* [1916] 1 KB 595 *per* Lord Reading CJ at p 614. In modern statutes brackets may be important. For example, in *Carver* v *Duncan* [1983] STC 310 Vinelott J said at p 339: 'The use of parentheses is at least an indication that the words in parentheses were intended as subordinate to — a qualification or gloss on — the preceding words which in themselves are the primary definition.'

THE WORD 'DEEMED'

It was an exaggeration to say at p **26** that the term 'deemed' is not used in the Capital Transfer Tax provisions. Certainly it does not have the importance that it once had for Estate Duty, and the draftsman of Part III of the Finance Act 1975 seems to have scrupulously avoided it, except in para 11(8) of Sched 5; but the word is used in the Finance Act 1976 — *see*, eg, ss 97, 105(1), 107(5) and 108(2) — and in subsequent legislation. One example is s 71(2) of the Finance Act 1978, which begins by providing that the section shall be deemed to have come into force on 11 April 1978. In *Egerton* v *IRC* [1983] STC 531 the taxpayers argued that a reference later in s 71(2) to the coming into force of the section must refer to the date of Royal Assent, but the Court of Appeal decided against them for the reasons explained at p 57, below.

Similarly, in *Sanderson* v *IRC* [1956] AC 491, where the phrase was 'where for the purposes of estate duty there pass', the House of Lords held that this included gifted shares which were 'deemed to pass'.

'THE SUBSTANCE OF THE TRANSACTION'

The new approach to tax avoidance schemes which was adopted by the House of Lords in *W T Ramsay Ltd* v *IRC* [1982] AC 300 and *IRC* v *Burmah Oil Co Ltd* [1982] STC 30 (*see* pp **37–40**) has been emphatically reaffirmed in *Furniss* v *Dawson* [1984] STC 153. This latest case shows that the principle is not limited to 'self-cancelling' schemes and that it may apply to deferment of tax liability as well as to outright avoidance. It seems that before the approach can operate there must be:

(1) a series of two or more steps that can be regarded as forming a single composite transaction, which may or may not have a legitimate commercial end;

(2) a scheme set up with the intention that it should follow through each of its stages;

(3) a scheme planned as a whole from the start, even though the preordained series of steps may be found in an informal arrangement or understanding rather than a binding agreement; and

(4) a step or steps inserted which have no business or commercial *purpose* (as opposed to *effect*) except to obtain a tax advantage.

If all these elements are present, the court will look at the end result and disregard the steps inserted for fiscal purposes.

Furniss v *Dawson* was a case on Capital Gains Tax, but there is little doubt that its principle is wide enough to cover Capital Transfer Tax. As to its possible application to gifts between spouses, *see* p 28 below.

Estate Duty (p 45–96)

The rate of interest has been reduced from 9 per cent to 6 per cent with effect from 1 December 1982 (SI 1982 No 1584).

Per an Inland Revenue press release of 3 May 1984, taper relief will not be given in future in relation to recapture charges on works of art.

Excluded Property (pp 103–107)

The paragraph at p **106** relating to 'Islanders' is now obsolete. Under s 12 of the Finance (No 2) Act 1983, s 45(1)(*c*) of the Finance Act 1975 ceases to have effect in relation to transfers of value made, or other events occurring, on or after 15 March 1983. Section 49 of the Finance Act 1977 has been repealed. The rule about Islanders' savings — para (iii) (*b*) at p **103** — is not affected.

'Transfer of Value' (pp 107–115)

As explained at pp **110–111**, the grant of a tenancy of agricultural property in the United Kingdom, Channel Islands or Isle of Man for use for agricultural purposes is not a transfer of value if the grantor makes it for full consideration in money or money's worth: FA 1981, s 97(1). Section 97(2) formerly said that 'agricultural property' in subs (1) had the same meaning as in Sched 14 to the Act. It has been retrospectively amended by FA 1984, s 107(3) with effect from 10 March 1981, and now reads:

> 'Expressions used in subsection (1) above and in Schedule 14 to this Act have the same meaning in that subsection as in that Schedule.'

The effect of the amendment is to apply s 107(1) of the 1984 Act, so that 'agricultural purposes' include the breeding and rearing of horses on a stud farm and the grazing of horses in connection with those activities (*see* p 16 below).

Free Estate (pp 122–129)

Damages for loss of expectation of life (*see* foot of p **124**) have been abolished by s 1(1) of the Administration of Justice Act 1982. Section 4(2) of that Act provides that the damages recoverable for the benefit of the estate shall not include 'any damages for loss of income in respect of any period after that person's death'. These provisions apply to deaths on or after 1 January 1983.

The result is that where a person dies instantaneously in an accident, the damages recoverable under the Law Reform (Miscellaneous Provisions) Act 1934 are normally limited to funeral expenses. Where the death is not instantaneous there may be a possibility of damages in respect of pain and suffering, including any suffering caused by the injured person's awareness that his expectation of life has been shortened.

Property Subject to a Contract (pp 129–130)

It was suggested at p **129** that para 5 of Sched 10 to the Finance Act 1975 applies to transfers on death in much the same way as s 3 of the Finance Act 1894. This is not now thought to be correct. The settlement made by the widow in *Re Harmsworth* [1967] Ch 826 was an exercise of her power to dispose of the property, not an exclusion or restriction of it, and para 5 would not be in point (cf p **1131**). As explained at p **1000**, property comprised in a settlement made for full consideration is not for that reason exempt from Capital Transfer Tax unless it comes within para 1(2) (*c*) of Sched 5 to the 1975 Act.

Initial Meaning of 'Transfer of Value' (pp 139–142)

It might have been mentioned here that, where a person gives consideration for an interest in possession in settled property, any question whether the giving of consideration is a transfer of value must be determined without regard to para 3(1) of Sched 5 to the Finance Act 1975: *see* s 69(7) of the Finance Act 1978. The operation of this rule is explained at pp **1086–1087**.

Intention of Gratuitous Benefit, etc (pp 143–156)

The meaning of 'shares or debentures not quoted on a

recognised stock exchange' is discussed at p **151**. Securities dealt in on the Unlisted Securities Market are not regarded as quoted for this purpose: *see* Statement of Practice 18/80 printed at p 497 of Vol 2.

What is said above in relation to *Re Harmsworth* applies equally to *Re Bateman* [1925] 2 KB 429, cited at p **154**. It is now thought that para 5 of Sched 10 to the Finance Act 1975 would not be relevant to a transaction of the *Bateman* type.

Free or Cheap Loans (pp 186–193)

The first paragraph on p **193** needs amendment as a result of s 9 of the Finance (No 2) Act 1983, under which the exemption for gifts to charities made on or after 15 March 1983 is not limited to £250,000 or any other figure (*see* p 29, below). The paragraph should now begin thus:

> 'Under s 117(5) loans to political parties within one year of death are not subject to the £100,000 limit in para 11 of Sched 6 to the 1975 Act. For the purposes of that paragraph and paras 10, 12 and 13 of Sched 6 (gifts to charities, for national purposes and for the public benefit) . . .'

Dispositions for Maintenance of Family (pp 207–215)

Paragraph 5 of Sched 9 to the Finance Act 1983 (a pre-consolidation amendment) inserts a reference to s 46(5) of the Finance Act 1975 (*see* p **213**) into para 4(10) of Sched 5 to the last-mentioned Act. The result is that references in s 46(5) to any property or to an interest in any property include references to part of any property or interest. It is understood that the Capital Taxes Office had already been interpreting s 46(5) in that way.

Alteration of Dispositions taking effect on Death (pp 215–235)

There is a misprint in the new version of s 47(1A) on p **226**. After the words 'settled by his will' there should be added 'and, within the period of two years after his death'.

In relation to deaths after 12 March 1984 s 47(1A) has been extended by FA 1984, s 103, inserting a new subs (1AA) into s 47 to cover events on which there is no charge to tax under the discretionary trust regime, eg, where property is distributed to charities. Accordingly, if property is settled by will and, within two years of the testator's death and before any interest in possession has subsisted in the property, an event occurs on which there would be a charge to tax under the discretionary trust regime apart from—

(*a*) FA 1982, s 115 (shares or securities becoming subject to employee trusts),

(*b*) FA 1982, s 119 (property becoming held for charitable purposes or by exempt bodies), or

(*c*) FA 1982, Sched 16, para 1(1) (property becoming comprised in maintenance funds for historic buildings),

the effect is the same as if the property had become held on those trusts immediately after the death. In most cases, therefore, the property will not be taxable on the death. A gift of more than £100,000 to a political party is an obvious exception.

Close Companies and Settled Property (pp 359-363)

FA 1984, Sched 21, para 14(2), removes the broad provision in FA 1975, Sched 5, para 24(1)(*a*), that references in s 39 to subs (1) are to have effect as references to para 24(2), and directs instead that:

(*a*) the reference in s 39(2) to subs (1) is to have effect as including a reference to para 24(2);

(*aa*) s 39 (3) is to apply to tax chargeable under para 24(2) as it applies to tax chargeable under s 39(1).

This more precise provision was no doubt considered desirable because, as noted at p 20 below, FA 1975, s 26(2), has been amended so as to restrict the liability for tax under para 24(2).

At the same time, FA 1984, Sched 21, para 14(3), makes FA 1975, Sched 5, para 24(5) (p **362**) apply for the purposes of 'this Part of this Act (except subsection (3) of section 23 and section 20(4) so far as relating to that subsection)'. The only purpose of the amendment is to facilitate consolidation: cf the note on employee trusts at p 58 below.

Employee Trusts (pp 363-368)

The limit of £1,250 a year mentioned in line 12 on p **365** has been increased by s 25 of the Finance Act 1983 to 'the relevant amount', meaning not less than £1,250 and not more than £5,000 but (subject to that) 10 per cent of the participant's salary.

The Cumulation Principle (pp 405-408)

Paragraph 3 of Sched 9 to the Finance Act 1983 makes a small pre-consolidation amendment to s 37(1)(*b*) of the Finance Act 1975. In its original form, s 37(1)(*b*) provided that to work out the rate of tax you had to aggregate the value of a chargeable transfer with the values previously transferred by chargeable transfers made by the same transferor. The resultant figure was usually known as the transferor's cumulative total. Section 93 of the Finance Act 1981 excluded gifts more than ten years old from the cumulative total, but the word 'previously' disappeared, so that on a literal construction the latest chargeable transfer might have had to be included twice. It is scarcely thinkable that the Revenue would have adopted that construction, or that any court would have supported them if they had, but para 3 of Sched 9 makes the point quite clear.

The reference in para 3 to 'previous chargeable transfers' does not mean that simultaneous chargeable transfers are not aggregated with each other. As stated at pp **420–421**, this is covered by s 43(3) of the 1975 Act, under which two or more chargeable transfers by the same person on the same day are taxed at the same rate as a single transfer of the same total value. Section 43(3) is subject to an exception where s 43(2) applies, in which case one or more transfers are treated as being previous to the other(s).

Alterations in Scales of Rates (pp 408–410)

Under s 8(1) of the Finance (No 2) Act 1983 indexation did not apply to chargeable transfers in the year beginning 6 April 1983. Instead, s 8(2) provided new scales of rates rather more generous than those which would have been available under s 91 of the Finance Act 1982. It increased the threshold to £60,000 with effect from 15 March 1983 and widened the rate bands so that the highest rates began at £2,650,000.

With effect from 13 March 1984 the Finance Act 1984, s 101(2), increased the threshold to £64,000 and reduced the top death rate from 75 per cent to 60 per cent, starting at £285,000. The lifetime rates became half the death rates all along the scale.

Paragraphs 2 to 7 of Sched 15 to the Finance Act 1980, summarised at pp **408–409**, apply to these new scales. The wording of some of those paragraphs has been slightly amended by FA 1984, Sched 21, para 23 (*see* p 90 below), but the meaning appears to be the same as before.

Rates on Death and within Three Years of Death (pp 410-413)

The new scales of death rates in the Finance (No 2) Act 1983, s 8(2), and the Finance Act 1984, s 101(2), are as follows.

Table 1—Rates on Death between 15 March 1983 and 12 March 1984

Slice of chargeable transfers which exceeds	*and does not exceed*	*Cumulative tax at minimum of range – ie, figure in col 1*	*Rate of tax on slice within the range*
£ thousand	£ thousand	£	per cent
60	80	nil	30
80	110	6,000	35
110	140	16,500	40
140	175	28,500	45
175	220	44,250	50
220	270	66,750	55
270	700	94,250	60
700	1,325	352,250	65
1,325	2,650	758,500	70
2,650	-	1,686,000	75

Table 1A—Rates on Death after 12 March 1984

Slice of chargeable transfers which exceeds	*and does not exceed*	*Cumulative tax at minimum of range – ie, figure in col 1*	*Rate of tax on slice within the range*
£ thousand	£ thousand	£	per cent
64	85	nil	30
85	116	6,300	35
116	148	17,150	40
148	185	29,950	45
185	232	46,600	50
232	285	70,100	55
285	—	99,250	60

Lifetime Rates (pp 417-419)

The new scales of lifetime rates under the Finance (No 2) Act 1983, s 8(2), and the Finance Act 1984, s 101(2), are as follows.

Table 2—Lifetime Rates between 15 March 1983 and 12 March 1984

Slice of chargeable transfers which exceeds	*and does not exceed*	*Cumulative tax at minimum of range – ie, figure in col 1*	*Rate of tax on slice within the range*
£ thousand	£ thousand	£	per cent
60	80	nil	15
80	110	3,000	17½
110	140	8,250	20
140	175	14,250	22½
175	220	22,125	25
220	270	33,375	30
270	700	48,375	35
700	1,325	198,875	40
1,325	2,650	448,875	45
2,650	—	1,045,125	50

Table 2A—Lifetime Rates after 12 March 1984

Slice of chargeable transfers which exceeds	*and does not exceed*	*Cumulative tax at minimum of range – ie, figure in col 1*	*Rate of tax on slice within the range*
£ thousand	£ thousand	£	per cent
64	85	nil	15
85	116	3,150	17½
116	148	8,575	20
148	185	14,975	22½
185	232	23,300	25
232	285	35,050	27½
285	—	49,625	30

Transfers Reported Late (pp 422-427)

Section 114(8) of the Finance Act 1976, mentioned at p **427**, was repealed by the Finance Act 1984, s 105(2) and Sched 23, Pt IX, with effect from 1 April 1983. Evidently the intention is to rely on s 105(1) of the 1984 Act, which covers fraud, wilful default or neglect by a settlor (*see* p 26, below).

Valuation of Unquoted Shares and Debentures (pp 447–477)

The figure of 20 per cent in the last paragraph on p **448** became 30 per cent with effect from 15 March 1983, as explained at p **17**, below.

Valuation of Freehold and Leasehold Property (pp 486–492)

In *Willett* v *IRC* (1982), 264 EG 257, the Lands Tribunal had to value a tenanted farm for Capital Transfer Tax on a death in May 1977. The tenant declined to give his age but was thought to be 66 or 67. There was a possibility that he might surrender his tenancy in return for money, but at the date of valuation negotiations for a surrender had been unsuccessful. The taxpayer's valuer took the tenant's expectation of life as 11.39 years and discounted the vacant-possession value for 12½ years on the assumption that vacant possession would not be obtained until a year or more after the tenant's death. The Tribunal agreed with the Revenue valuer that the tenant would probably retire in his lifetime and that the vacant-possession value (estimated at £66,000) could reasonably be discounted for eight years. After adding the value of the rent for those eight years, the resultant figure was increased by about 10 per cent to reflect the value to the sitting tenant. The value so determined was £39,000, as against £28,000 estimated by the taxpayer and £45,000 by the District Valuer.

The Lands Tribunal remarked that in valuing property under s 38 of the Finance Act 1975 it is right to assume that it is suitably lotted (*see Ellesmere* v *IRC* [1918] 2 KB 735) — a point which neither valuer had taken directly into account. In fact the tenant was persuaded to surrender his tenancy and the property was sold in four lots to two buyers for a total of £126,750, but that was 17 months after the death and prices had risen.

Tax Deposit Certificates (p 493)

A new prospectus (Series 6) for Certificates of Tax Deposit was introduced with effect from 11 October 1982. The main differences from the old series are that—

(1) the rates of interest earned will be realigned with current rates on each anniversary of the deposit, rather than on the second and fourth anniversaries only;
(2) the rates of interest may vary according to the size of the deposit. It is expected that deposits of £100,000 or over (which must be remitted direct to the Bank of England) will earn higher rates.

'Value Transferred' (pp 503–509)

Because of s 8 of the Finance (No 2) Act 1983 the grossing table on p **508** applies only to lifetime transfers between 9 March 1982 and 14 March 1983. Grossing tables for later transfers are given below.

Table 3 — Grossing table for lifetime transfers between 15 March 1983 and 12 March 1984

Net	*Multiplier*	*Gross*
£		£
60,000	20/17	60,000
77,000	40/33	80,000
101,750	5/4	110,000
125,750	40/31	140,000
152,875	4/3	175,000
186,625	10/7	220,000
221,625	20/13	270,000
501,125	5/3	700,000
876,125	20/11	1,325,000
1,604,875	2	2,650,000

Table 3A—Grossing table for lifetime transfers after 12 March 1984

Net	*Multiplier*	*Gross*
£		£
64,000	20/17	64,000
81,850	40/33	85,000
107,425	5/4	116,000
133,025	40/31	148,000
161,700	4/3	185,000
196,950	40/29	232,000
235,375	10/7	285,000

Farm Cottages (p 521)

Under FA 1984, s 107(2), the existing provisions of FA 1975, Sched 10, para 12, become para 12(1) and are followed by a new para 12(2) which reads:

> 'Expressions used in sub-paragraph (1) above and in Schedule 14 to the Finance Act 1981 have the same meaning in that sub-paragraph as in that Schedule.'

The effect is that the phrases 'agricultural property' and 'agricultural purposes' in para 12 must be read in conformity with FA 1984, s 107(1), under which the breeding and rearing of horses on a stud farm and the grazing of horses in connection with those activities are taken to be agriculture (*see* p 16 below). The amendment is retrospective to 10 March 1981.

Scottish Agricultural Leases (pp 521–523)

Section 98 of the Finance Act 1981 and s 97 of the Finance Act 1982 apply only to tenancies held by an individual or held jointly by individuals, and not to tenancies held by a partnership or a company. Joint occupation under a joint tenancy is not in Scots law the same thing as a tenancy held by a partnership: cf *Haddo House Estate Trustees* v *Davidson* [1982] SLT (Land Court) 14, a case on notice to quit.

Reduction in Value of Agricultural Property (pp 523–542)

The 20 per cent relief for tenanted land in para (*b*) on p **525** was increased to 30 per cent by s 10(2) of the Finance (No 2) Act 1983. The increase has effect in relation to transfers of value made, and other events occurring, on or after 15 March 1983.

As noted at p **526**, casual lettings, eg, of grazing rights for less than a year, do not destroy the lessor's occupation of the land let. But where there is a series of such lettings the conditions of para 3 of Sched 14 do not in strictness appear to be satisfied unless the land was occupied for the purposes of agriculture during the short periods when it was unlet (*see* 'CTT News', April 1984, p 71, and June 1984, p 86).

The reference to *Sudeley* v *A-G* at p **528** is not now in point, because FA 1975, Sched 5, para 22 (*see* p **1126**) applies with effect from 26 July 1984.

STUD FARMS

Under FA 1984, s 107(1), the breeding and rearing of horses on a stud farm and the grazing of horses in connection with those activities are taken to be agriculture for the purposes of FA 1981, Sched 14. Similarly, any buildings used in connection with those activities are farm buildings within the meaning of Sched 14, para 1(2). The section is retrospective and, like Sched 14 itself, has effect from 10 March 1981.

The clause which became s 107 was inserted into the Bill at the report stage. According to the Financial Secretary to the Treasury the clause was not a concession but was to remove any doubt that agricultural relief was available to stud farmers. He explained that relief was given where stud farming was ancillary to general farming, and that there was no satisfactory reason why relief should be withheld from an enterprise which was engaged solely in stud farming.

It is thought that there was not much doubt about the position before the Act was passed. The breeding, rearing and grazing of horses for use on a farm appears to be agriculture, while the breeding of horses for sport (eg, racing or show-jumping) is evidently not agriculture: *Normanton (Earl)* v *Giles* [1980] 1 WLR 28.

In most cases, of course, the point is academic. If a stud farm did not qualify for agricultural relief it would qualify for business relief at 50 per cent. But the Financial Secretary argued that s 107 was necessary because:

(1) Business relief is avoidable only on the disposal of a business or an interest in a business, not the individual assets of a business. Agricultural relief is more flexible and is available on the disposal of part of a farm.

(2) If the owner of land uses it for a stud farm in partnership with others, business relief would be available at 30 per cent, but agricultural relief might be 50 per cent, depending on the terms of the arrangement.

(3) Business relief is available only where the activity is carried on for gain. If a stud farm has consistently made losses, the Inland Revenue may not be easily convinced that it is being carried on with a view to profit.

He added that the words 'stud farm' were included in s 107 as a means of excluding hobby owners whose horse breeding is incidental to their ownership of the animals or who keep or graze horses on just a few acres of land around their houses. But there is no definition of 'stud farm' in the Act. It was suggested in debate that a stud farm might exist without the presence of a stallion at the stud, and the Financial Secretary promised to consider whether the (non-existent) definition was adequate.

Reduction in Value of Business Property (pp 542–558)

MINORITY SHAREHOLDINGS IN UNQUOTED COMPANIES

The 20 per cent relief in para (3) on p **544** was increased to 30 per cent by s 10(1) of the Finance (No 2) Act 1983 in relation to transfers of value made, and other events occurring, on or after 15 March 1983. The reference to 20 per cent on p **542** applies only to transfers and events before that date.

SETTLED PROPERTY USED BY A LIFE TENANT

It is noted at p **547** that before 10 March 1981 settled property could not qualify for the 30 per cent relief (under para 3(1) (*c*) of Sched 10 to the Finance Act 1976) if used for the purposes of a business carried on solely by the life tenant. That statement remains unchallenged, notwithstanding the anomaly that relief *was* available if the life tenant carried on the business in partnership. However, in *Finch* v *IRC* [1984] 3 WLR 212 the Court of Appeal held that the business relief under para 3(1)(*a*) (30 per cent at the date of death, but now 50 per cent) was available.

The facts were as follows. The deceased was tenant for life of an estate of 5,500 acres, of which 1,845 were in hand. A claim for agricultural relief in respect of 1,000 acres of the land in hand was agreed. 446 of the remaining 845 acres were woodland subject to relief under Sched 9 to the Finance Act 1975. Of the balance of 399 acres, 142 were occupied by the deceased for less than two years before his death. The claim for business relief was limited to the remaining 257 acres.

The notional transfer of value which took place on the death in September 1977 included the business of farming and forestry carried on by the deceased. The value attributable to that business had to be reduced by 30 per cent under paras 2(1) and 3(1) (*a*) of Sched 10 to the 1976 Act. At first sight the value attributable to the business could not include any of the settled land, which was not in fact part of the business. But the trustees relied on para 6 of Sched 10, which says that the value of a business is its net value under para 14(2) of Sched 4 to the 1975 Act. Paragraph 14(2) says that the net value of a business is the value of the assets used in the business (including goodwill) reduced by the amount of any liabilities incurred for the purposes of the business.

The majority of the Court of Appeal, adopting a literal interpretation of paras 6 and 14(2), held that the trustees were entitled to relief. Oliver and O'Connor LJJ could see no reason for departing from the plain words of the Act. O'Connor LJ said: 'Where the property consists of a business, I think it is obvious that any land or building, machinery or plant, used wholly or mainly for the purposes of the business, are part of the business, always remembering that they must themselves be part of the transfer of value.'

Vinelott J in the lower court had been of a contrary opinion, holding that if para 14(2) were construed as the trustees contended there would be an overlap between sub-paras (*a*) and (*c*) of para 3(1). The interest of a deceased partner in the assets of a partnership would include land owned by him and used by the partnership (though not in the ordinary sense an asset of the partnership) and the land itself would attract relief under para 3(1)(*c*). The existence of this overlap, the judge said, afforded an indication that para 3(1)(*a*) was not intended to extend to such land.

Oliver and O'Connor LJJ were of the opinion that there was no such overlap. They thought that the phrase 'the entire business' at the end of para 14(2) must refer to the partnership property and not to the property of any individual partner that might be used in the business. Whether this reasoning is correct seems a little doubtful, because the first limb of para 14(2) provides that the net value of a business is the value of the assets used in the business, reduced by the liabilities. Even in the case of a partnership the farmland is, as Oliver LJ said, 'the one asset without which the business cannot be carried on at all'.

Oliver LJ mentioned four anomalies that arose on the Crown's construction of the statutory provisions:

(1) If the deceased had been the absolute owner instead of the life tenant in possession, the property would have been relevant business property under para 3(1)(*a*).

(2) If the business had been carried on by a company controlled by the deceased, or by a partnership of which he was a member, it would have qualified under para 3(1)(*c*).

(3) If the business had been comprised in the settlement, or had belonged to a company the controlling shares in which

were comprised in the settlement, the land would have been part of the relevant business property.

(4) If a life tenant formed a farming partnership with another person, relief in respect of the land would depend on the accident of whether the other partner survived him.

Oliver LJ said that his construction avoided these anomalies, and O'Connor LJ said he did not think that that construction produced any anomalies. But this seems not to be so, because in the fourth example above the business relief is apparently 30 per cent under para 3(1)(*c*) if the other partner survives, while if he dies first the relief on the life-tenant's death is 50 per cent under para 3(1)(*a*) — assuming that the death is before 10 March 1981 and that the agricultural relief is not available. Further, it seems that before that date the land qualified for interest-free instalments if the other partner died first, but not if he survived. Finally, if the life-tenant's business is insolvent, it appears that for the purposes of business relief the net liabilities have to be deducted from the value of the settled land, though in fact they fall on the life-tenant's non-business assets.

Though the four judges who heard the case were equally divided, the court refused leave to appeal to the House of Lords.

There remains the question of the effect (if any) of para 3(1)(*d*), inserted by FA 1981, s 100. Three possibilites are suggested:

(*a*) The 30 per cent relief under para 3(1)(*d*) supersedes the 50 per cent relief under para 3(1)(*a*).

(*b*) The 30 per cent is to be added to the 50 per cent, making 80 per cent altogether.

(*c*) The 50 per cent relief overlaps the 30 per cent relief, so that para 3(1)(*d*) has no effect at all.

The official view on this question is not yet known.

MINIMUM PERIOD OF OWNERSHIP

The reference to *Sudeley* v *A-G* at p **550** is not now in point, because FA 1975, Sched 5, para 22 (*see* p **1126**) applies with effect from 26 July 1984.

VALUATION

FA 1976, Sched 10, para 6, is explained at p **551**. Its meaning was further considered in *Finch* v *IRC,* above.

Deduction of Liabilities: General Rules (pp 559-568)

The words 'a transferor's estate' in FA 1975, Sched 10,

para 1(1) (p **559**), have been replaced by the words 'a person's estate': FA 1984, Sched 21, para 16.

Liabilities on Death (pp 569–576)

FA 1984, s 96(8) and Sched 9, para 14, insert new clauses (*e*) and (*f*), printed at p 73 below, into FA 1975, Sched 10, para 9(1). These provide for the allowance of income tax on death in respect of offshore income gains and deemed disposals of deep discount securities.

Tax Liabilities on Lifetime Transfers (pp 576–578)

A capital gains tax liability postponed under FA 1984, Sched 14, may become due when a close relative of the 'beneficiary' benefits from the trust. If the close relative pays the tax the payment is treated, under para 16 of the Schedule, as made in satisfaction of a liability of his and so not a transfer of value.

Liability for Tax: Gifts Inter Vivos (pp 580–582)

At p **582** the authors express the view that 'property' in FA 1976, s 119, does not include property directly or indirectly representing it. This is now confirmed by FA 1984, Sched 21, para 2, which inserts the words '(except subsection (8))' into FA 1975, s 25(10).

Exceptions from Liability (p 586)

The references in para (3) to 'charity' and '£250,000' do not apply to gifts made after 14 March 1983: F(No 2)A 1983, s 9, discussed at p 29, below.

FA 1984, Sched 21, para 3, makes two amendments to FA 1975, s 26(2):

(*a*) The words from the beginning to 'respectively, and' cease to have effect. Consequently s 26(2) no longer affects national heritage property or woodlands.

(*b*) The words 'or by virtue of paragraph 24(2) of Schedule 5 to this Act' are added at the end. This prevents the liability from being wider where tax is charged under para 24(2) than where it is charged under s 39(1) (*see* pp **355** and **359–360**).

Certificates of Discharge (pp 592–593)

The last paragraph on p **593** seems to be wrong and should be deleted. If the deceased's taxable estate is increased by an order of court under the Inheritance (Provision for Family and Dependants) Act 1975, para (ii) on that page meets the situation.

The 'taxable estate' includes property in which the deceased had an interest in possession under a settlement. It makes no difference that the order of court increased the value of the deceased's free estate and not that of the settled property. Trustees of settlements should therefore be wary in cases in which the Inheritance Act may apply, bearing in mind the court's discretion to extend the time limit in s 4 of that Act (*see* p **238**).

Incidence of Tax (pp 595–626)

FREE REAL ESTATE

The rule in para (4) on p **600** has been abrogated by s 13(1) of the Finance (No 2) Act 1983, with the result that testamentary expenses now include Capital Transfer Tax on free real estate in the United Kingdom unless the will shows a contrary intention. Section 13(1) substitutes for s 28(1) of the Finance Act 1975 a new s 28(1) and (1A), which reads as follows:

'(1) Where personal representatives are liable for tax on the value transferred by a chargeable transfer made on death, the tax shall be treated as part of the general testamentary and administration expenses of the estate, but only so far as it is attributable to the value of property in the United Kingdom which—

(*a*) vests in the deceased's personal representatives, and

(*b*) was not, immediately before the death, comprised in a settlement.

The provision made by this subsection shall have effect subject to any contrary intention shown by the deceased in his will.

(1A) Where any amount of tax paid by personal representatives on the value transferred by a chargeable transfer made on death does not fall to be borne as part of the general testamentary and administration expenses of the estate, that amount shall, where occasion requires, be repaid to them by the person in whom the property to the value of which the tax is attributable is vested.'

Paragraph 8(*b*) of Pt II of Sched 1 to the Administration of Estates Act 1925, mentioned in the fourth line of p **601**, has been repealed (along with the corresponding Northern Irish provision) by Pt II of Sched 2 to the Finance (No 2) Act 1983 with effect from 26 July 1983.

It had already been decided in *Re Dougal* [1981] STC 514, cited at p **601**, that heritable property in Scotland should not bear its own tax unless the will so directed. The new s 28(1) extends the *Dougal* principle to real property in England, Wales and Northern Ireland. It is understood that this legislation was discussed in advance with The Law Society and other professional bodies, and there is reason to expect that it will be generally welcome. The following points are worthy of note:

(1) Under s 13(3) the new rule applies only to deaths on or after 26 July 1983. In relation to earlier deaths, as explained at pp **601–602**, opinion is divided on whether the *Dougal* principle would be adopted by an English court. In practice, by extra-statutory concession, the Capital Taxes Office in England has given executors the option of following or not following *Dougal* and paying tax accordingly.

(2) The new rule applies only to property in the United Kingdom. Free property outside the United Kingdom, whether movable or immovable, must continue to bear its own tax unless the will directs otherwise. This is understood to be so even in Scotland, though on the face of it the reasoning of *Dougal* would seem capable of extending to a specific bequest of foreign property. Where legacies are payable out of a mixed fund of British and foreign property they must, in the absence of a contrary intention, bear their due proportion of the tax on the foreign property (*see* p **605**).

(3) The new rule has no application to settled property over which the deceased exercised a general power of appointment by will — para (1) at p **600**.

(4) Real property in the United Kingdom appears to be the only exception to the rule that property subject to the Inland Revenue charge bears its own tax unless the will directs otherwise.

(5) For the meaning of 'any contrary intention shown by the deceased in his will' *see* pp **614–617**. As noted at p **615**, it has been held to be not enough that the will contains a direction to pay testamentary expenses out of particular property or charges the property with such expenses. There must also be an intention to exonerate some other class of property from the liability; but the court will usually infer an intention to exonerate unless the property is undisposed of by the will or passes under some other title. Thus a direction charging real property with its own tax is arguably ineffective if there is undisposed-of personalty out of which the tax can be paid.

(6) The new s 28(1A) in effect restates the old s 28(1) as interpreted in *Dougal*.

(7) Statement of Practice E17, noted at p **601** and printed at p 494 of Vol 2, is superseded.

APPORTIONMENT

In *Re Hogg* ('Law Society's Gazette', 9 November 1983, p 2838) a testator had directed his executors to pay all duties in the nature of Estate Duty leviable on all property passing on his death under his will, out of capital in exoneration of income, notwithstanding any rule of equity to the contrary. The court held that the purpose of the direction was primarily to exclude the rule in *Allhusen* v *Whittell* (1867) LR 4 Eq 295 (*see* p **608**), under which Capital Transfer Tax and the interest on it would have formed a single debt to be apportioned between capital and income. As the rule was excluded, it followed that the tax, along with the interest, must be paid out of capital.

The result will be the same, so far as free estate in the United Kingdom is concerned, if a testator directs payment of testamentary expenses out of capital in exoneration of income. Interest on tax is as much a testamentary expense as the tax itself: FA 1975, s 28(1) and (8), as amended by F(No 2)A 1983, s 13.

TAX ON FOREIGN PROPERTY

The citation of *Re Sebba, Lloyds Bank Ltd* v *Hutson* at p **617** should have been [1959] Ch 166 or [1958] 3 WLR 605.

ADJUSTING THE BURDEN OF TAX

The original s 28(1) of the Finance Act 1975, mentioned in the last paragraph on p **624**, has been replaced by a new s 28(1) and (1A) quoted in full above under the heading of 'Free Real Estate'. Section 28(1A) still uses the words 'where occasion requires'. The meaning of this phrase, as interpreted in *Christie's Trustees* v *Christie's Trustees* [1943] SC 97, is explained at pp **624–625**; but that case was distinguished in *Re Dougal,* above. It is thought that what is said at pp **624–625** is still correct, subject to deletion of the word 'personal' in the first line of p **625**.

The statement at p **625** that the s 28(4) charge does not include the costs of settling the tax is plainly wrong, in view of the last sentence on p **626**. Section 28(8) of the Finance Act 1975, which is the authority for that sentence, has been amended by s 13(2) of the Finance (No 2) Act 1983 with effect from 26 July 1983. It now says: 'References in this section (except subs (2)) to tax include references to interest on tax and, in subss (3) to (5), to costs properly incurred in respect of tax.' One may therefore assume that the references to tax in subss (1), (1A) and (2) do *not* include the costs of paying it. The new s 28(8) is not restricted to *deaths* after 25 July 1983, because s 13(3) refers also to other events on which tax is chargeable after that date.

Accounts (pp 628–634)

The words 'relevant property' in para 2(2A) of Sched 4 to the Finance Act 1975 have been replaced by the words 'appropriate property': Finance Act 1983, Sched 9, para 4. This avoids any possible confusion with 'relevant property' as defined by s 102 of the Finance Act 1982 for the purposes of the discretionary trust regime. The word 'relevant' in line 13 of p **630** should now be 'appropriate'.

Where the death is on or after 1 April 1983, the gross value of £25,000 in para (*b*) on p **631** is increased to £40,000 and the £1,000 in para (*d*) is increased to £2,000 by the Capital Transfer Tax (Delivery of Accounts) (No 3) Regulations 1983 (SI 1983 No 1039) and the Capital Transfer Tax (Delivery of Accounts) (Scotland) (No 2) Regulations 1983 (SI 1983 No 1040). These regulations relate to England and Wales and Scotland and came into operation on 1 September 1983. The regulations for Northern Ireland (SI 1981 No 1441, printed at pp 395–396 of Vol 2) were brought into line by SI 1983 No 1911 with effect from 1 February 1984.

In England and Wales, with effect from 1 September 1983, a new flat-rate probate fee of £80 has replaced the *ad valorem* scale for estates between £25,000 and £40,000 net. As a general rule, where an estate is subject to a flat-rate fee no account will be due, and *vice versa*. But this is not always so. For instance, an estate might be below the £40,000 limit but not an 'excepted estate' because it contained settled property. An account would be required even though a flat-rate probate fee would be charged.

In Scotland no new confirmation fee structure is proposed to accompany the new 'excepted estate' limit. No changes are being made in the rules governing applications for confirmation to an estate. The inventory must therefore continue to be completed and presented to the Sheriff Clerk in the normal way.

Inspection for Valuation (p 636)

Under the Criminal Justice Act 1982, ss 37, 38(1), (6) and (8), 46(1) and (4) (*a*) and 75, the £20 fine in para 11(2) of Sched 4 to the

Finance Act 1975 has become a fine not exceeding level 1 on the standard scale (currently £25).

Instalments (pp 638-643)

In relation to chargeable transfers on or after 15 March 1983, the provisions for payment of tax by eight yearly or sixteen half-yearly instalments (in FA 1975, Sched 4, paras 13, 14 and 15) are replaced by provisions for payment by ten equal yearly instalments: F(No 2)A 1983, s 11(1). This fits in with the ten-yearly charge on discretionary trusts (p **1137**). Where the instalment option is available, one instalment is payable in each year of the period between one ten-year anniversary and the next.

With effect from 15 March 1983 also, s 11(2) increases to £20,000 the figure of £5,000 in para 13(3) of Sched 4 — *see* para (5) at pp **638** and **641**. This seems fair, in view of inflation since 1975 and the 30 per cent discount given by s 10 of the same 1983 Act — *see* p 17, above.

As noted at p **639**, there was no definition of 'land' in FA 1975. FA 1984, Sched 21, para 5, now provides that:

> '"land" includes buildings and other structures, land covered with water, and any estate, interest, easement, servitude or right in or over land; but does not include any estate, interest or right by way of mortgage or other security'.

The words up to the semi-colon are the same as in Sched 1 to the Interpretation Act 1978 and are therefore omitted from the CTT Act, s 272.

Interest on Tax (pp 643-645)

With effect from 1 December 1982 the rate of interest on unpaid tax (and on repayments of tax) is 6 per cent if the chargeable transfer was made on death and 8 per cent in other cases: SI 1982 No 1585. In view of para 19(2) of Sched 4 to the Finance Act 1975, the lower rate applies also to the extra tax payable on death when a transferor dies within three years of the transfer.

The words 'to any person' and 'of that person' in FA 1975, Sched 4, para 19(4) (*see* the second paragraph on p **645**) have been repealed by FA 1984, Sched 21, para 8, and Sched 23, Pt IX, as being unnecessary.

Acceptance of Property in Satisfaction of Tax (pp 645-649)

A new edition of the Treasury booklet *Capital Taxation and the National Heritage* was published in July 1983 at a price of £2.50.

Appendices B and C to the 1980 booklet (mentioned at p **646**) are Appendices A and B to the 1983 booklet, and Chapter 14 of the 1980 booklet (p **647**) is Chapter 12 of the 1983 booklet. The first sentence on p **648** should now be: '(iii) Is the object of especial importance for the study of some particular form of art, learning or history?'

As stated at p **648**, ss 50 and 51 of the Finance Act 1946 were repealed by the National Heritage Act 1980. The reference to them in s 78(4) (*b*) of the Finance Act 1976 has now been deleted by para 6 of Sched 9 to the Finance Act 1983.

Corrections (pp 650–652)

Paragraph 23(3) of Sched 4 to the Finance Act 1975 (p **651**) provides that, in any case of fraud, wilful default or neglect by a person liable for tax, proceedings for recovery can be brought at any time within six years after the fraud, default or neglect comes to the knowledge of the Board. Section 105 of the Finance Act 1984 extends this provision to cover fraud, wilful default or neglect by a settlor where tax is chargeable under the discretionary trust regime.

The new section applies for example, where the settlor failed to disclose chargeable transfers, so that the trust's cumulative total (*see* p **1143**) appeared to be less than it actually was. It has effect in relation to any fraud, etc, coming to the knowledge of the Board after 31 March 1983.

Recovery of Tax (pp 653–655)

PERSONAL LIABILITY

In *IRC* v *Stannard* [1984] STC 245 the question arose whether an executor was personally liable for Capital Transfer Tax payable on the death of the testator. If so, the court would make an order against him in the *de bonis propriis* form, so that execution could issue against his own assets. If he was not personally liable, the order would be in the *de bonis testatoris* form, and execution would in the first instance issue only against the assets of the testator.

Scott J could find nothing in FA 1975, s 25(5), which justified limiting the liability of a personal representative to liability in a representative capacity only. Section 27(1), which limited his liability to the assets which he had received as personal representative or might have so received but for his own neglect or default, was concerned with the extent of the liability, not its character.

The learned judge cited *Dymond's Death Duties*, 15th edition, p 927, which under the heading 'Enforcement of Liability — Personal Liability' says:

> 'Every person who is made accountable for Estate Duty becomes a Crown debtor, and his goods and estate are accordingly liable to satisfy the debt (*Berry* v *Gaukroger* [1903] 2 Ch 116).'

In his judgment the same was true of Capital Transfer Tax. The order was therefore made in the *de bonis propriis* form.

EVIDENCE

A certificate by an officer of the Board that tax or interest on tax is due and has not been paid is sufficient evidence in any proceedings for the recovery of the tax or interest: FA 1975, Sched 4, para 36A, inserted by FA 1984, s 106(2).

COUNTY COURTS

Where proceedings for recovery of tax are taken in a county court (para (1) at p **654**) an officer of the Board who is authorised by the Board to do so may address the court: FA 1984, s 106(1).

PROCEEDINGS IN SCOTLAND

Under FA 1984, s 106(1), tax and interest within the sum specified in s 35(1)(*a*) of the Sheriff Courts (Scotland) Act 1971 (currently £1,000) may be sued for and recovered in the sheriff court. An officer of the Board so authorised by the Board may address the court.

Notice of Determination (pp 656–657)

Under FA 1975, Sched 4, para 6(6), references to transfers of value are to be construed as including references to occasions of charge under the discretionary trust regime, but recapture charges in respect of woodlands or national heritage property are not expressly mentioned. On the principle that 'the machinery must be made to fit' (*see* p **19**) it is thought that the court would treat para 6 as covering such charges; but FA 1984, Schedule 21, para 6, removes all doubt by amending subpara (6) so that it reads:

> 'References in this paragraph to transfers of value or to the values transferred by them shall be construed as including references to—
>
> (*a*) disposals on which tax is chargeable under paragraph 2 of Schedule 9 to this Act,

(*b*) chargeable events by reference to which tax is chargeable under section 78 of the Finance Act 1976,

(*c*) occasions on which tax is chargeable under section 82 of the Finance Act 1976 or under Chapter II of Part IV of the Finance Act 1982,

or to the amounts on which tax is then chargeable.'

Appeals to the Special Commissioners (pp 658–659)

It will usually simplify and shorten the hearing before the Special Commissioners if the facts can be agreed beforehand (*see* pp 503–504 of Vol 2). However, the parties need to be very careful when agreeing a statement of facts, because it will be binding on them; they cannot go behind it and contend that the facts were otherwise: *Symons* v *Weeks and others* [1983] STC 195.

The fee of £1 for stating a case (p **659**) is increased to £25 by FA 1984, Sched 22, para 6. The paragraph will come into operation on such day as the Lord Chancellor may by order made by statutory instrument appoint.

Appeals Direct to the High Court (pp 659–660)

The definition of 'High Court' in Northern Ireland as a judge of the High Court (FA 1975, Sched 4, para 44) has been repealed by FA 1984, Sched 21, para 9, and Sched 23, Pt IX.

Transfers between Husband and Wife (pp 665–672)

As noted at p **667**, the limit of the exemption for spouses domiciled overseas kept pace with the tax threshold of £15,000, £25,000, £50,000 or £55,000 between 27 March 1974 and 14 March 1983. It remains at £55,000 notwithstanding the increase of the threshold to £64,000 in FA 1984.

The question has been raised (eg, in 'Law and Tax Review', March 1984, p 33, and 'CTT News', April 1984, p 64) as to whether a gift of £3,000 by a husband to his wife, to enable her to use her annual exemption by giving the money to a child, would be affected by the recent decision in *Furniss* v *Dawson* (p 5 above). It is thought that the position remains as stated at pp **198–199**, except that it may not now matter whether the transactions are 'associated operations' as defined in FA 1975, s 44.

LEGITIM

Interest on a repayment of tax under FA 1976, s 123(2) (p **670**) has been made free of income tax by FA 1984, Sched 21, para 22. This brings s 123(2) into line with s 122(8) — *see* foot of p **242**.

Gifts to Charities (pp 672–676)

The limit of £250,000 in para (*b*) on p **672** has been removed by s 9(1) of the Finance (No 2) Act 1983 with effect from 15 March 1983. The result is that all gifts to charities are exempt, even though made on death, unless they come within the exceptions at pp **682–687**.

Gifts to Political Parties (pp 676–678)

The eight political parties in the list on p **677** qualified for exemption as a result of the general election in June 1983, and so did the Social Democratic Party. Three other parties (all Irish) each got one seat in the House of Commons but failed to get the necessary 150,000 votes.

Gifts for National Purposes, etc (pp 678–680)

To the list of heritage bodies on p **678** there should now be added the Historic Buildings and Monuments Commission for England (Finance Act 1983, s 46).

Gifts for the Public Benefit (pp 680–682)

Paragraph (*e*) at p **681** is strictly interpreted. Where property is given as a source of income for the upkeep of other qualifying property, only the income can be used. If a source of capital is required, the answer is to set up a maintenance fund (*see* pp **822–834**).

Application for the exemption should be made in the first instance to the Capital Taxes Office, not the Treasury. If the body concerned has not been previously approved, the applicant should submit all relevant documents, such as trust deeds and (if the body is incorporated) its memorandum and articles of association, with full details of its assets, expected income and forecast expenditure.

Partial Exemption (pp 687–711)

The £250,000 limit for gifts to charities mentioned at pp **687** and

691 has (as noted above) been removed with effect from 15 March 1983.

In consequence of s 8 of the Finance (No 2) Act 1983, Table 4C at p **695** applies only to deaths between 9 March 1982 and 14 March 1983. Tables for later deaths are given below.

Table 4D — Grossing table for deaths brtween 15 March 1983 and 12 March 1984

Net	Fraction	Gross
£		£
60,000	10/7	60,000
74,000	20/13	80,000
93,500	5/3	110,000
111,500	20/11	140,000
130,750	2	175,000
153,250	20/9	220,000
175,750	5/2	270,000
347,750	20/7	700,000
566,500	10/3	1,325,000
964,000	4	2,650,000

Table 4E — Grossing table for deaths after 12 March 1984

Net	Fraction	Gross
£		£
64,000	10/7	64,000
78,700	20/13	85,000
98,850	5/3	116,000
118,050	20/11	148,000
138,400	2	185,000
161,900	20/9	232,000
185,750	5/2	285,000

In connection with Examples 2, 5, 7, 9, 10, 13 and 14 at pp **692–706** it should be remembered that in Scotland a specific bequest of heritable property does not bear its own tax unless the testator so directs: *Re Dougal* [1981] STC 514. In England, on deaths before 26 July 1983, the Capital Taxes Office gives executors the option of following *Dougal* in relation to real property and paying tax accordingly. The rule in *Dougal* has been made statutory for later deaths (*see* pp 21–22, above).

Death on Active Service, etc (pp 743–746)

Because of changes in military law the list of Women's Services in para 1(3) of Sched 7 to the Finance Act 1975 is no longer needed for the purposes of the exemption. Paragraph 1(3) and the relevant words in para 1(2) have been repealed by the Armed Forces Act 1981, Sched 5.

Applications for exemption in respect of members of the British Armed Forces should be addressed to:

Defence Secretariat 15
Ministry of Defence
Main Building
Whitehall
London SW1A 2HB

Overseas Pensions (pp 746–747)

FA 1975, Sched 7, para 4(2)(*b*), has been amended by FA 1984, Sched 21, para 15. In place of the words 'which is or forms part of a colony, protectorate, protected state or United Kingdom trust territory' we now have 'which, at the time when the fund was established, was or formed part of a colony (within the meaning of Schedule 1 to the Interpretation Act 1978), protectorate, protected state or United Kingdom trust territory'.

National Heritage Property (pp 799–834)

As noted above with reference to pp **645–649**, a new edition of the Treasury booklet *Capital Taxation and the National Heritage* mentioned at p **799** was published in July 1983. The reference at p **801** to Chapter 7 of the booklet relates to Chapter 6 of the new edition, which incidentally explains that trees and underwood may share in the exemption if they contribute to the scenic or scientific interest of the land on which they stand. The definition of 'historically associated object' at the foot of p **801** (para 8.4 of the old booklet) has been modified, and there is now no reference to 'a considerable period (usually many generations)'. According to para 7.4 of the new edition the object must have a close association with a particular building and make a significant contribution, whether individually or as part of a group or scheme of decoration, to the appreciation of that building or its history.

Where an object is lent to a public collection for special exhibitions, para 5.7 of the booklet says that the duration of the loan need not exceed six months in any two-year period (as stated at p **804**) or such longer loan and period as would be reasonable in appropriate cases, except that the duration need not exceed 25 per cent of the period. The paragraph also gives examples of what is meant by 'exhibitions which are properly organised and meet adequate security standards'.

Private treaty sales to heritage bodies (pp **807–808**) are free not only from Capital Transfer Tax but also from Capital Gains Tax, and this is taken into account when calculating the 25 per cent or 10 per cent 'douceur' (as illustrated in Appendix A to the Treasury booklet). Such sales are also relieved from Value Added Tax.

According to para 11.1 of the booklet, a private treaty sale to a heritage body will always be financially more advantageous to the owner than a sale in the open market involving a charge to tax. This statement has been challenged in an article in *The Conveyancer* ([1984] Conv 221). If the property is agricultural land of outstanding scenic interest, it may pay better not to claim conditional exemption, but to pay tax with the benefit of agricultural relief and then sell in the open market. The Treasury booklet evidently assumes that conditional exemption has already been granted.

SIX YEAR'S OWNERSHIP

The words in para (*b*) on p **805** 'or its value was left out of account for tax under s 31 or 34 of the Finance Act 1975 or for Estate Duty under s 40 of the Finance Act 1930 (or its Northern Irish equivalent)' can now be deleted. The relevant part of FA 1976, s 76(3)(*b*), has been repealed by FA 1984, Sched 21, para 20, and Sched 23, Pt IX. As the death in question must have occurred before 7 April 1976, the property will qualify for exemption under s 76(3)(*a*).

MAINTENANCE FUNDS

Paragraphs 10.7 to 10.13 of the old Treasury booklet, mentioned at p **824**, are replaced by paras 9.7 to 9.14. In the old para 10.11 the Treasury said that the trustees could not use the fund to finance new buildings or to acquire fresh land, but the new para 9.12 accepts that the purchase of additional farm land to generate a higher income for the fund may qualify as an improvement. Improvements should be undertaken only after making proper provision for the maintenance of the heritage property.

The accounts to be furnished to the Treasury (p **825**) should include an adequate record of any accumulations of income made during the life of the fund.

The second limb of FA 1982, s 94(6) (p **833**), which treats s 94(2) and (3) as having been in force when designations, undertakings and acceptances were made under FA 1976, s 84(6), is repealed by FA 1984, Sched 21, para 24, and Sched 23, Pt IX, as being unnecessary.

The provisions of FA 1982, Pt IV, relating to maintenance funds are split between Chapter I (ss 93–95) and Chapter II (s 117 and Sched 16). Consequently ss 120–124 applied to Sched 16 but not to ss 93–95. This somewhat schizophrenic situation has been put right by FA 1984, Sched 21, paras 25 and 26, which provide that ss 120(1), 121(1) and (2), 122(1), 123 and 124 are to apply for the purposes of ss 93 and 94. Sections 120(1), 121(1) and (2) and 123 are also to apply for the purposes of FA 1976, ss 81, 82 and 82A.

Exempt Government Securities (pp 836–841)

Section 104(2) of the Finance Act 1984 inserts a new sub-para (2AA) after para 3(2A) of Sched 7 to the Finance Act 1975 with effect from 15 March 1983. Under this, para 3(2A) does not apply where a reversionary interest in property expectant on the termination of a qualifying interest in possession subsisting under the first settlement was settled on the trusts of the second settlement before 10 December 1981.

Section 104(2) does the same for para 3(2A) as s 104(1) does for s 121(1) of the Finance Act 1982 (*see* p 50, below). It is not retrospective to 9 March 1982 because in some rare cases the taxpayer may be better off if the property is treated as remaining in the first settlement.

The suggestion at p **840** that para 3(2A) was not strictly necessary was rejected by the court in *Minden Trust (Cayman) Ltd* v *IRC* [1984] STC 434. Warner J distinguished *IRC* v *Brandenburg* [1982] STC 555 and said that it was not permissible to apply para 11(4) of Sched 5 in the interpretation of para 3(2) of Sched 7, because —

(1) it is not necessary, for the purpose of applying para 6(2) of Sched 5, to identify the settlement there referred to;
(2) it must be right to go to para 11(11) before applying paras 6(4) and 8;
(3) para 11(4) does not apply for the interpretation of

para 11(11) — it applies only for the interpretation of paras 6 to 10;

(4) the effect of para 11(11) is that 'excluded property' is excluded from 'the property comprised in a settlement' referred to in para 6(2), but the excluded property is necessarily part of 'the settled property' referred to in para 3(2) of Sched 7. The two are not therefore co-extensive.

It is understood that the Revenue are appealing against this decision.

Islanders' Savings (p 842)

It should be noted that National Savings Income Bonds are *not* excluded property within para 5 of Sched 7 to the Finance Act 1975.

Visiting Forces (pp 842–843)

With effect from 1 January 1983 the words 'citizen of the United Kingdom and colonies' on p **842** are replaced by 'British citizen, British Dependent Territories citizen or British Overseas citizen': British Nationality Act 1981, s 51(3). A brief summary of that Act is given at pp **947–948**.

'Islanders' (pp 850–853)

Section 45(1)(*c*) of the Finance Act 1975 has ceased to have effect in relation to transfers of value made, and other events occurring, on or after 15 March 1983: Finance (No 2) Act 1983, s 12. Section 49 of the Finance Act 1977 has been repealed by Pt II of Sched 2 to the 1983 Act. Consequently, the text at pp **850–853** applies only to transfers of value and other events before 15 March 1983.

Situs of British Government Securities (p 857)

National Savings Income Bonds are securities registered on the National Savings Stock Register and are situate in the United Kingdom.

Domicile and Residence (pp 869–884)

As indicated above, s 45(1)(*c*) of the Finance Act 1975 has been repealed with effect from 15 March 1983. Paragraph (*c*) at the top of p **870** is therefore obsolescent. So also are:

(1) para (*c*) on p **879**;

(2) the references to limb (*c*) of s 45(1) on pp **879-884**;

(3) the reference in para (6) on p **880** to s 49(1) of the Finance Act 1977, which has now been repealed.

The result is that the Channel Islands and the Isle of Man are treated as foreign countries for the purposes of Capital Transfer Tax, except that they enjoy privileges in respect of agricultural property (pp **523-542**) and national savings (p **842**).

FA 1984, Sched 21, para 4, amends FA 1975, s 45(1), by inserting the words '(and not elsewhere)' after the words 'as domiciled in the United Kingdom' (p 879, line 5), and provides that s 52(3) shall cease to have effect. This makes it clear that the notional domicile in the United Kingdom is in substitution for, and not additional to, the domicile under ordinary law. Section 51(3) is repealed as being unnecessary.

Double Taxation Relief (pp 889-994)

THE OECD MODEL CONVENTION

The OECD Draft Double Taxation Convention on Estates and Inheritances, referred to at p **896** and later pages as the 1966 Model Convention, has been replaced by the 1982 Model Double Taxation Convention on Estates and Inheritances and on Gifts. As the name indicates, the main new feature is that taxes on gifts *inter vivos* are now included within the scope of the Convention.

The new Model does not have any direct effect on Capital Transfer Tax, but indirectly it may affect it in two ways:—

(*a*) future double taxation conventions entered into by the United Kingdom will probably conform more closely to the new Model than past conventions have done;

(*b*) the new Model (and the commentaries on its articles) may affect the interpretation of existing conventions. The introductory report by the OECD Committee on Fiscal Affairs contains the following passage:

'The Committee on Fiscal Affairs has examined the problem of conflicts of interpretation which could arise as a result of changes in the text of the Articles or of the Commentaries. The Committee considers that existing conventions should, as far as possible, be interpreted in the spirit of the new Commentaries, even though the

> provisions of existing conventions do not yet contain the more precise wording of the 1982 Estate Tax Model. Member countries wishing to clarify their positions in this respect may do so by means of an exchange of letters between competent authorities in accordance with the mutual agreement procedure. Even in the absence of such an exchange of letters, these authorities would use the mutual agreement procedure to secure this interpretation in particular cases.'

It is therefore thought that a concise explanation of the new Model may be of interest to readers of *Dymond*. Its text is printed at pp 94–106, below.

Chapter I: Scope

Article 1 says that the Convention shall apply (*a*) to estates and inheritances where the deceased was domiciled, at the time of his death, in one or both of the Contracting States, and (*b*) to gifts where the donor was domiciled, at the time of the gift, in one or both of the States.

This is broadly equivalent to Article 1 of the Convention with the Netherlands (p **960**), except that there is no mention of settlements. Our conventions with other countries are not expressly limited by reference to the domicile of the deceased or the donor.

Article 2 deals with the taxes covered and has four paragraphs, the first of which applies the Convention to taxes on estates and inheritances and on gifts imposed by a Contracting State or its political subdivisions or local authorities. There are, of course, no such local taxes in the United Kingdom; and, as noted at p **939**, the Convention with the United States does not extend to taxes levied by individual American states.

The second paragraph of Article 2 says that taxes on estates and inheritances include taxes imposed by reason of death in the form of taxes on the *corpus* of the estate, of taxes on inheritances, of transfer duties, or of taxes on *donationes mortis causa*; and taxes on gifts include taxes imposed on transfers *inter vivos* only because such transfers are made for no, or less than full, consideration. Thus, for example, Capital Gains Tax charged on a gift of property would not be covered, because that tax would be imposed just the same if the property had been sold.

The third paragraph lists all the taxes covered by the Convention when it is signed. The fourth paragraph extends it to any identical or substantially similar taxes which are imposed afterwards, and also requires the competent authorities to notify each other, at the end of each year, of changes which have been made in their respective taxation laws.

None of the conventions made by the United Kingdom contains anything resembling the first and second paragraphs of Article 2. The Double Taxation Agreement with India (which is not a member of the OECD) includes only the third paragraph. Other conventions made by the United Kingdom include the third and fourth paragraphs, except that the obligation to notify changes is found only in the conventions with the United States and the Netherlands and omits the words 'at the end of each year'.

Chapter II: Definitions

Paragraph 1 of Article 3 provides for only two definitions. The first says that, unless the context otherwise requires, the term 'property which forms part of the estate of, or of a gift made by, a person domiciled in a Contracting State' includes any property the devolution or transfer of which, under the law of a Contracting State, is liable to a tax covered by the Convention. This is a new definition, which has no counterpart in the 1966 Draft. It is not found in any United Kingdom conventions, for the simple reason that they do not use the term quoted.

The second definition is of the term 'competent authority' in each State.

Paragraph 2 of the Article provides that any term not defined in the Convention shall, unless the context otherwise requires, have the meaning which it has under the law of each State concerning the taxes to which the Convention applies.

All the conventions made by the United Kingdom contain the equivalent of para 2, along with a string of definitions which vary from one convention to another.

Paragraph 1 of Article 4 defines the term 'person domiciled in a Contracting State' as meaning any person whose estate or whose gift, under the law of that State, is liable to tax therein by reason of the domicile, residence or place of management of that person or any other criterion of a similar nature. However, the term does not include any person whose estate or whose gift is liable to tax in that State only in respect of property situated therein.

This paragraph is quite different from the 1966 Draft and is similar to the definition of 'resident of a Contracting State' in the 1977 Income Tax Model. In United Kingdom conventions made since 1975 a person is domiciled in the United Kingdom if he is domiciled there in accordance with its law or is treated as so domiciled for the purposes of a tax which is the subject of the convention. Only the Convention with the Netherlands contains a proviso (*see* p **962**) similar to the second sentence of para 1 of Article 4.

Paragraph 2 of Article 4 provides four rules for determining the status of an individual who under para 1 is domiciled in both States. Similar rules are to be found in all United Kingdom conventions except those with India and Switzerland, and they are discussed in some detail at pp **909–913**. As noted in the last paragraph on p **949**, the Convention with the United States is slightly different.

Paragraph 3 provides that where under para 1 a person other than an individual is domiciled in both States it shall be deemed to be domiciled in the State where its place of effective management is situated. This has no counterpart in United Kingdom conventions, because Capital Transfer Tax is a tax on individuals only.

Chapter III: Taxing Rules

Immovable Property

Paragraph 1 of Article 5 says that immovable property which forms part of the estate of, or of a gift made by, a person domiciled in a Contracting State and which is situated in the other Contracting State may be taxed in that other State.

The United Kingdom conventions with South Africa, the United States, the Netherlands and Sweden adopt the simpler formula of the 1966 Draft: 'Immovable property may be taxed in the Contracting State in which such property is situated.' It is not clear why the more long-winded 1982 version was thought to be advantageous. Perhaps it is intended, along with the definition in Article 3, to cater for taxes which are not strictly taxes on property: *see* the last two sentences of the first paragraph on p **929**.

Paragraph 2 defines 'immovable property' in terms similar to those of the South African and United States conventions. The proviso that debts secured by mortgage or otherwise shall not be regarded as immovable property is not in Article 5 itself but is mentioned in the Commentary as an optional addition to the Article. As noted at pp **963** and **971**, the Dutch and Swedish conventions also provide that 'immovable property' includes an interest in the proceeds of sale of land which is held on trust for sale.

Paragraph 3 says that para 1 shall also apply to immovable property of an enterprise and to immovable property used for the performance of professional services or other activities of an independent character. The conventions with South Africa, the United States, the Netherlands and Sweden have a similar provision, which refers to 'the performance of independent personal services'. Presumably the meaning is the same.

Business Property

Under para 1 of Article 6, movable property of an enterprise which forms part of the estate of, or of a gift made by, a person domiciled in a Contracting State, which is the business property of a permanent establishment situated in the other State, may be taxed in that other State. Paragraphs 2 to 5 explain what is meant by 'permanent establishment'. Paragraph 6 extends the rule to movable property used for the performance of professional services or other activities of an independent character and pertaining to a fixed base situated in a Contracting State.

Apart from the reference to estates and gifts this Article 6 is much the same as Article 6 of the Dutch Convention (p **963**), but there is no exception for ships, boats and aircraft and no mention of partnerships. The South African and United States conventions contain additional provisions (*see* pp **931** and **952**) dealing with dependent and independent agents and associated companies: these are taken from the 1977 Income Tax Model.

Ships and Aircraft

Article 7 of the 1966 Draft contained provisions about ships, boats and aircraft similar to those of the South African, Dutch and Swedish conventions (*see* pp **932**, **963** and **971**). There is no such provision in the 1982 Model, because the Committee on Fiscal Affairs decided that Article 6 (business property) ought to apply. The United Kingdom has reserved its position on this point.

Other Property

Article 7 of the 1982 Model provides a residual rule that property, wherever situated, which forms part of the estate of, or of a gift made by, a person domiciled in a Contracting State, and not dealt with in Articles 5 and 6, is taxable only in that State.

This is similar to Article 8 of the Dutch Convention (p **964**). Article 5(1)(*a*) of the United States Convention has broadly the same effect but is subject to the exceptions in the later paragraphs of that Article (*see* pp **950–952**). Article 5(1) of the South African and Swedish conventions (pp **929** and **970**) allows the other State to tax the property if the deceased or the donor was domiciled there within the ten years immediately preceding the death or gift, and there are other exceptions more or less resembling those of the United States Convention. The Dutch Convention has a domicile-within-ten-years rule in Article 11(1) (p **965**), but it is limited to nationals of the other State.

Deduction of Debts

Article 8 of the Model lays down six rules for the deduction of debts.

1. Debts especially secured on any immovable property, or represented by the acquisition, conversion, repair or upkeep of any such property, are to be deducted from the value of that property.
2. Subject to para 1, debts pertaining to business property in Article 6 are to be deducted from the value of that property.
3. Other debts are to be deducted from the value of property in Article 7.
4. If a debt exceeds the value of the property from which it is deductible in a Contracting State under paras 1 and 2, the excess is to be deducted from the value of any other property taxable in that State.
5. Any excess still remaining in one Contracting State after the deductions in paras 3 and 4 is to be deducted from the value of the property taxable in the other State.
6. Where paras 1 to 5 would oblige one State to deduct debts to an extent greater than that provided for under its law, those paragraphs apply only to the extent that the other State is not obliged to deduct the same debts under its own law.

These rules work in two directions:

(i) they sometimes require a State to deduct debts which under its own law would not be deductible; and
(ii) they sometimes give a State the right to decline the deduction of debts which under its own law would be deductible.

If a State because of its domestic law cannot exercise its right to decline to deduct debts, Article 8 may lead to a double deduction of debts. The United Kingdom is in this uncomfortable position, because its conventions have effect only so far as they provide *relief* from Capital Transfer Tax (or for determining the *situs* of property

— an outmoded concept): Finance Act 1975, Sched 7, para 7(1). Accordingly, all five of the conventions made since 1975 say merely that, in determining the amount on which tax is to be computed, permitted deductions shall be allowed under the law in force in the Contracting State in which the tax is imposed.

Article 8 does not give any definition of what is to be regarded as a deductible debt. According to the Commentary, an obligation which would not in any circumstances be regarded as a deductible debt in a Contracting State will not become deductible simply by the provisions of the Article.

Chapter IV: Methods of Eliminating Double Taxation

The Commentary explains that there are two leading principles for eliminating double taxation by the State in which the deceased or the donor was domiciled.

1. The principle of exemption, under which the State of domicile does not tax the property which under the Convention may be taxed in the other State (State of *situs*). There are two main methods:

   (*a*) The property taxable in the State of *situs* is not taken into account at all by the State of domicile. This is called 'full exemption'.

   (*b*) The property taxable in the State of *situs* is not taxed in the State of domicile, but its value is taken into account in determining the rate of tax on other property. This is called 'exemption with progression'.

2. The principle of credit, under which the State of domicile taxes the property but allows a deduction for tax paid in the State of *situs*. Here again there are two main methods:

   (*a*) The State of domicile allows all the tax paid on the property in the State of *situs*. This is called 'full credit'.

   (*b*) The deduction given by the State of domicile is restricted to that part of its own tax which is attributable to the property taxable in the State of *situs*. This is called 'ordinary credit'.

The Model Convention offers two alternative Articles, 9A giving 'exemption with progression' and 9B giving 'ordinary credit'. None of the conventions made by the United Kingdom adopts the exemption method, and so only Article 9B will be considered here. Its first paragraph says that the State of domicile shall allow as a deduction from the tax calculated according to its law an amount equal to the tax paid in the other State on any property which, in relation to the same event and in accordance with the Convention, may be taxed in that other State. The third paragraph provides that the deduction is not to exceed that part of the tax of the State of domicile which is attributable to the property in respect of which the deduction is to be allowed.

United Kingdom conventions follow these principles, but the wording of the relevant article varies widely from one convention to another. Some provisions are reciprocal, while others have separate rules for each of the two countries concerned. There are usually special provisions for settled property.

Paragraph 2 of Article 9B requires the State of domicile to allow an amount equal to the tax paid in the other State on a previous gift, to the extent that such a deduction has not been allowed under para 1 at the time of the gift. This operates in relation to tax on later gifts by the donor and on his death, where for any reason a full allowance was not made in respect of the previous gift, eg, because the tax in the State of domicile was less than in the State of *situs*. It covers cases where the domicile was unchanged and cases where the donor changed his domicile from one Contracting State to the other between the gifts or between the gift and the death. A primitive counterpart to para 2 may be found in Article 12(4)(*c*) of the South African Convention (p **935**) or Article 13(4)(*b*) of the Dutch Convention (p **967**), but the rule is limited to gifts within three years of death.

Chapter V: Special Provisions

It is not very obvious why this chapter is headed 'Special Provisions'. One might think it could equally well have been called 'General Provisions'; for there appears to be nothing special or peculiar about its five articles. Even the Irish Convention (pp **902–920**), which in most respects diverges from the Model, includes four of these articles with only slight changes of wording.

Article 10, which deals with non-discrimination, is similar to Article 24 of the 1977 Income Tax Model. It prevents discrimination against the nationals (as defined in para 2) of the other State and against stateless persons. Notwithstanding Article 2 it applies to taxes of every kind and description.

As noted at p **972**, the Swedish Convention says nothing about non-discrimination, for the good reason that the subject is already covered by the Income Tax Convention. The other post-1975 conventions all have non-discrimination articles, which are based on the Income Tax Model but relate only to capital taxes. The definition of 'national(s)' is always put into Article 3, and stateless persons are not mentioned. In the United States, where the Estate Tax is based substantially on nationality, Article 10 does not protect a British national from being taxed as a non-resident alien.

Article 11 is concerned with the mutual agreement procedure and resembles Article 16 of the Dutch convention (*see* p **967**). It provides also that any agreement reached shall be implemented notwithstanding any time limits in the domestic laws of the Contracting States, and that the competent authorities may consult together for the elimination of double taxation in cases not provided for in the Convention.

Article 12 deals with the exchange of information and closely resembles the corresponding articles of the Irish and Dutch conventions (*see* p **920**). There is no mention of the prevention of fraud or the administration of statutory provisions against legal avoidance of tax, as there is in the conventions with South Africa, the United States and Sweden. The Article specifically provides against restriction by Article 1, so that the information may include particulars of persons not domiciled in either State.

Article 13 directs that nothing in the Convention shall affect the fiscal privileges of diplomatic agents or consular officers under the general rules of international law or under special agreements. All the conventions made by the United Kingdom since 1975 have a similar article.

Article 14 provides for extension of the Convention to any part of the territory of either State which is specifically excluded from the application of the Convention or to any State or territory for whose international relations either State is responsible, which imposes similar taxes. There are corresponding articles in the pre-1975 conventions with India, Switzerland, France and Italy, and in the post-1975 Convention with the Netherlands.

Chapter VI: Entry into Force and Termination

Under Article 15, the Convention is to enter into force when it has been ratified and the instruments of ratification have been exchanged.

Under Article 16, the Convention is to remain in force until terminated. Either State may terminate it through diplomatic channels by giving notice at least six months before the end of any calendar year after a specified year.

All the United Kingdom conventions contain articles similar to Articles 15 and 16. Those made before 1975 were to remain in force for a minimum period of three years, which is increased to five years for conventions made after 1975.

SOUTH AFRICAN DONATIONS TAX

This tax is briefly described at p **926**, where para (*b*) speaks of an exemption for gifts up to 15,000 rand made to each of the donor's children. This is not quite accurate. The exemption was for gifts to children with a limit of 15,000 rand multiplied by the number of children. The 1983 Act increases the limit to 20,000 rand with effect from 1 April 1983. Thus, if a taxpayer has four children, he may give a total of 80,000 rand tax-free to any one or more of them, less an amount equal to any previous gifts which were exempt under this provision.

The exemption ceiling for the casual gifts in para (*h*) has been increased to 5,000 rand for the year of assessment ended on or after 1 March 1983.

Meaning of 'Settlement' and Related Expressions (pp 998–1015)

The words 'for his own use or benefit' in the last line but five on p **998** presumably mean much the same as the words 'for the deceased's own use and benefit' in s 7(1) of the Finance Act 1894. This is discussed at pp **68–69**.

MORE THAN ONE SETTLOR; MORE THAN ONE SETTLEMENT

By FA 1984, Sched 21, para 10, the application of FA 1975, Sched 5, para 1(8) (p **1004**), has been extended to FA 1975, s 22(2) and (3) (reverter to settlor or settlor's spouse — pp **1087–1092**) and s 24(3) (reversionary interests — pp **246–249**), and FA 1982, ss 93 and 94 (maintenance funds — pp **822–834**). This fills some evident gaps in the legislation.

The decision in *Bond* v *Pickford* mentioned at pp **1008–1009** has been upheld by the Court of Appeal at [1983] STC 517. Slade LJ said that there was a crucial distinction to be drawn between (*a*) powers to alter the presently operative trusts of a settlement which expressly or by necessary implication authorise the trustees to remove assets altogether from the original settlement (without rendering any person absolutely beneficially entitled to them), and (*b*) powers of this nature which do not confer such authority on the trustees. He referred to these as 'powers in the wider form' and 'powers in the narrower form'. The first of the 'two fairly typical cases' mentioned by Lord Wilberforce in *Roome* v *Edwards* [1982] AC 279 was an example of exercising a power in the narrower form, and the second was an example of exercising a power in the wider form. The power in *Bond* v *Pickford* was indubitably in the narrower form, and its exercise did not create a new or separate settlement. Oliver LJ said that the appropriated funds remained subject to trusts which the settlement itself envisaged, and the settlement trustees remained the trustees of them with the same powers and provisions as affected the remainder of the settled funds.

Interests in Possession Generally (pp 1021-1022)

With effect from 28 January 1983 the reference to ss 3 and 4 of the Insurance Companies Act 1981 at the end of the second paragraph on p **1022** should be read as a reference to ss 3 and 4 of the Insurance Companies Act 1982.

Types of Interest in Possession (pp 1040-1043)

It was suggested at p **1042** that the decision in *Re Weir's Settlement Trusts* [1971] Ch 145 might not apply to Capital Transfer Tax, because the beneficiary in that case did have 'a present right of present enjoyment' which would be an interest in possession for the purposes of the tax. This question was discussed in *Moore* v *IRC* [1984] STC 236, in which the settlor was, from the date of the settlement until his death, the sole beneficiary in existence under a discretionary trust. There was a possibility that the class of beneficiaries would increase if he married, but in the events he alone was entitled to the income.

Peter Gibson J held that, where the class of objects of a discretionary trust is not closed, the sole existing object cannot claim an immediate entitlement to income. It is always possible that before a reasonable time for distribution of the income has elapsed another object will come into existence. Any other conclusion would be unsatisfactory, because there would be a series of charges to tax as a result of the class increasing to two or dropping again to one. Further, if the right of the trustees to withhold income depends on their knowledge of the circumstances, there could be further charges as the position known to the trustees changed from time to time.

It was accepted by both sides, and by the learned judge, that if the class of objects had been closed (as in the *Weir* case) the sole remaining object would have had an interest in possession for the purposes of the tax: *Re Nelson* [1928] Ch 920.

In *Swales* v *IRC* [1984] STC 413 a fund was to be held on discretionary trusts until a child of the settlor's daughter attained 21 or being female married ('the vesting event'). In 1970 the trustees executed a deed of appointment directing that the income of the fund be held on trust for the daughter absolutely. In 1976 the daughter's eldest child attained 21. The Revenue claimed that the appointment could not come into effect until the vesting event occurred. The trustees contended that the appointment took effect subject to the vesting event occurring and the daughter then being alive, and that they were bound to pay her the intermediate income by virtue of the Trustee Act 1925, s 31(1)(ii). It was held that the trustees were right, that the daughter had an interest in possession before 1976, and that there was no capital distribution within FA 1975, Sched 5, para 6(2), on the vesting day. But Nicholls J rejected an alternative argument of the trustees that an arrangement for payment of income to a beneficiary by a standing order on the trustees' bank account was analogous to an arrangement for her to occupy a house forming part of the trust property: cf *Sansom* v *Peay* [1976] 1 WLR 1073, mentioned at p **1076**. The standing order conferred no right on the beneficiary in respect of the trust income to which it related.

Transfer of Interest Treated as Termination (pp 1074–1076)

In line 18 on p **1076** there should be a bracket before 'treated' as well as after 'bankrupt'.

Occupation of Property by Beneficiary Rent-free (pp 1076–1078)

The reference at the end of para (3) on p **1077** should of course be read as s 108(1)(*b*) of the Finance Act 1982.

'Surviving Spouse Exemption' (pp 1092–1116)

FA 1975, s 22(4), cited at p **1093**, has been amended by FA 1984, Sched 21, para 1, so that it now reads:

> 'In determining for the purposes of this Part of this Act the value of the estate, immediately before his death, of a person

whose spouse (or former spouse) died before 13th November 1974, there shall be left out of account the value of any property which, if estate duty were chargeable on the later death, would be excluded from the charge by section 5(2) of the Finance Act 1894 (relief on death of surviving spouse).'

FA 1975, Sched 5, para 4(7), has been amended by FA 1984, Sched 21, para 11, which inserts the words '(or surviving former spouse)' after the words 'surviving spouse'.

The meaning of s 22(4) appears to be unchanged, but the amendment to para 4(7) gives statutory sanction to the official practice mentioned in the first paragraph on p **1094**.

The citation of *A-G* v *Dodington* on p **1113** should be [1897] 2 QB 373.

Chargeable Transfer during Administration Period (pp 1126–1127)

The ambit of FA 1975, Sched 5, para 22, has been broadened by FA 1984, Sched 21, para 13. The rule now applies for the purposes of the tax generally instead of only for Sched 5.

Commencement of Settlement (pp 1135–1136)

Section 123 of the Finance Act 1982 was altered (perhaps rather hastily) at the report stage. The text at p **1135** inadvertently describes s 123 as it appeared in the original Bill. In fact it reads: 'Property which becomes comprised in a settlement in pursuance of a will or intestacy shall for the purposes of this Chapter be taken to have become comprised in it on the death of the testator or intestate (whether it occurred before or after the passing of this Act).'

Section 123 is at first sight hard to reconcile with s 120 of the 1982 Act in a case where a testator gives his spouse a life interest in his estate with remainder on discretionary trusts. Section 120 then treats the property as becoming comprised in a separate settlement made by the spouse when the life interest ceases, but s 123 treats it as becoming comprised in the settlement on the death of the testator. It is suggested that s 123 provides a general rule, and that s 120 makes an exception to that rule, so that s 120 should prevail.

Under FA 1984, Sched 21, para 25, ss 120(1) and 123 apply not only for the purposes of FA 1982, Pt IV, Chapter II, but also for those of ss 93 and 94 of the 1982 Act and FA 1976, ss 81, 82 and 82A.

The Ten-Yearly and Exit Charges (pp 1137-1141)

The words 'immediately before a ten-year anniversary' in FA 1982, s 107, are officially construed as referring to the day before the anniversary, and so the property has to be valued as on that day.

It should be noted that income in the hands of the trustees at a ten-year anniversary is subject to the ten-yearly charge. There is nothing in s 107 of the Finance Act 1982 corresponding to s 108(5), which forbids any exit charge in respect of a payment which is (or will be) income of any person for any of the purposes of income tax. Trustees can therefore save tax by distributing as much income as possible before the ten-year anniversary.

The 30 per cent grossing table in Vol 2, mentioned at p **1141**, applies only to distributions made between 9 March 1982 and 14 March 1983. For later distributions the tables below may be used.

Distributions made between 15 March 1983 and 12 March 1984 — grossing up at 30 per cent of full rate

Net cumulative total			*Reduced rate on slice per cent*	*Tax payable*			
£		£		£	£		£
60,000	—	79,100	4.5	Nil	+ 9/191	for each £ over	60,000
79,100	—	107,525	5.25	900	+ 21/379		79,100
107,525	—	135,725	6	2,475	+ 3/47		107,525
135,725	—	168,362.50	6.75	4,275	+ 27/373		135,725
168,362.50	—	209,987.50	7.5	6,637.50	+ 3/37		168,362.50
209,987.50	—	255,487.50	9	10,012.50	+ 9/191		209,987.50
255,487.50	—	640,337.50	10.5	14,512.50	+ 21/179		255,487.50
640,337.50	—	1,190,337.50	12	59,662.50	+ 3/22		640,337.50
1,190,337.50	—	2,336,462.50	13.5	134,662.50	+ 27/173		1,190,337.50
Over £2,336,462.50			15	313,537.50	+ 3/17		2,336,462.50

Distributions made after 12 March 1984 — grossing up at 30 per cent of full rate

Net cumulative total			*Reduced rate on slice per cent*	*Tax payable*			
£		£		£	£		£
64,000	—	84,055	4.5	Nil	+ 9/191	for each £ over	64,000
85,055	—	113,427.50	5.25	945	+ 21/379		84,055
113,427.50	—	143,507.50	6	2,572.50	+ 3/47		113,427.50
143,507.50	—	178,010	6.75	4,492.50	+ 27/373		143,507.50
178,010	—	221,485	7.5	6,990	+ 3/37		178,010
221,485	—	270,112.50	8.25	10,515	+ 33/367		221,485
Over £270,112.50			9	14,887.50	+ 9/91		270,112.50

Rate of Exit Charge (pp 1150–1156)

The last paragraph on p **1152** states inaccurately that property becoming settled on a death is taken to have become comprised in the settlement immediately before the death. As noted above, s 123 of the Finance Act 1982 was amended at the report stage and provides that property settled by a will or intestacy is taken to have become comprised in the settlement on the death of the testator or intestate. However, the purpose of the section is unchanged, so that the last four lines on p **1152** and the first seven lines on p **1153** remain valid.

Property Becoming Held for Charitable or Public Purposes (pp 1156–1157)

A further example may help to illustrate the operation of s 119(3) of the Finance Act 1982. Suppose that the trustee of a discretionary trust holds 5,500 out of 10,000 shares in a private company and that a holding between 50 and 60 per cent is considered to be worth £10 a share, while one between 49 and 50 per cent is worth only £6 a share. If the trustee distributes all the shares to individual beneficiaries, tax will be payable on £55,000. The following scheme might be devised to save tax.

(1) Distribute 499 shares to individual beneficiaries. Tax is payable on £4,990.

(2) Give 2 shares to a charity. No tax is payable, apart from s 119(3).

(3) Distribute the remaining 4,999 shares to individual beneficiaries. Tax is payable on £29,994.

So, if it were not for s 119(3), only £34,984 would be taxed instead of £55,000.

In order to apply s 119(3), we must consider what tax would be charged on the gift to charity apart from s 119. The calculation would be:

	£
Value of 5,001 shares at £10	50,010
Less value of 4,999 shares at £6	29,994
	20,016

As the value of 2 shares in the hands of the charity is perhaps £2, tax is payable under s 119(3) on the excess, viz £20,014. The device is therefore useless for saving tax.

Initial Interest of Settlor or Spouse (pp 1157-1159)
Property Moving between Settlements (pp 1159-1161)

It might have been helpful to mention under these headings s 122 of the Finance Act 1982, which is discussed at pp **1139-1140**. Section 122 is designed to prevent the avoidance of tax by exploitation of ss 120 and 121. Suppose, for example, that *A*, who is domiciled outside the United Kingdom, settles foreign property on discretionary trusts for a short period with remainder to himself. *B* buys *A*'s reversion after 9 December 1981 and settles it on discretionary trusts. Under s 121 the property is treated as remaining comprised in *A*'s settlement, and apart from s 122 it would be excluded property and not liable to tax. Under s 122 it is *not* taken to be excluded property unless *B* also was domiciled outside the United Kingdom when he made his settlement.

With effect from 15 March 1983, FA 1984, s 104(1), adds a new subs (3) to FA 1982, s 121. The result is that s 121(1) does not apply where a reversionary interest in property expectant on the termination of a qualifying interest in possession subsisting under the first settlement was settled on the trusts of the other settlement before 10 December 1981. This removes an unintended element of retrospection from s 121. Under the previous law and practice, as explained at pp **1160-1161** and **1223**, if the reversion was settled before 10 December 1981 the property would not have been treated as remaining comprised in the first settlement.

Where the reversion was settled before 10 December 1981 and fell into possession before 15 March 1983 the taxpayer is in no way prejudiced, because he can elect to be taxed under the old law as explained at p **1164**.

Under FA 1984, Sched 21, para 25, ss 120(1) and 121(1) and (2) apply not only for the purposes of FA 1982, Pt IV, Chapter II, but also for those of FA 1982, ss 93 and 94, and FA 1976, ss 81, 82 and 82A.

Meanings of Basic Terms (pp 1173-1188)

The decision in *IRC* v *Trustees of Sir John Aird's Settlement (No 2)*, mentioned at pp **1172** and **1175**, which was concerned with the meaning of 'capital distribution', was upheld by the Court of Appeal at [1984] STC 81.

The Crown argued that FA 1975, Sched 5, para 6(2), was in the nature of a timeless definition, so that a transaction effected before 13 March 1975 could still be 'a capital distribution treated as made' even though it was not taxable as such. Nourse J had held that the words 'shall' and 'becomes' in para 6(2) made it a provision of a futuristic character, which could not apply to anything done before the Act came into force. The Court of Appeal unanimously agreed with the Crown that little weight could be attached to the word 'shall' read by itself; but the majority considered that the word 'becomes', while apt to refer to the present and the future, was *prima facie* not apt to refer to a past event. This *prima facie* construction was supported by the context, because:

(1) The Crown's reading of para 6(2) in a timeless sense necessitated reading into para 6(4) some such words as 'made on or after 13 March 1975', while the alternative construction did not make it necessary to read any words into para 6(4).

(2) The Crown was seeking to attach a broad interpretation to para 6(2) so as to bring transactions effected between 27 March 1974 and 12 March 1975 within the admittedly retrospective provisions of para 8(2)(*a*), by which they would not otherwise be caught. In contrast, payments within para 6(1) were caught by para 8(2)(*a*) because of the admittedly timeless defintion in para 11(7). The broad interpretation of para 6(2) was not required to make the charging provisions of para 6 perfectly workable. Against that background, and in view of the presumption against retrospective legislation, the court should lean towards the narrower construction.

The reference in the fifth paragraph on p **1183** to 'para 11(1)' should be to para 11(10). The reference halfway down p **1185** to 'p 660' should be to pp **1176–1177**.

The Charge of Tax and the Value Chargeable (pp 1188–1190)

As noted at p **1189**, FA 1975, Sched 5, para 11(5), says that the amount of any distribution payment which is a capital distribution shall be taken, except for the purposes of para 6(4)(*a*), to be the amount on which tax is chargeable in respect of it. The defendants in *IRC* v *Trustees of Sir John Aird's Settlement (No 2)*, mentioned above, argued in the lower court that for that reason the amount of any distribution payment made before 13 March 1975 must be nil, because no tax was chargeable. Nourse J did not have to decide the point, but he said that in his judgment it could not possibly be correct, and it was not pursued in the Court of Appeal. The answer seems to be that a distribution payment made before 13 March 1975 cannot in any circumstances be a capital distribution.

Rates of Tax: the Applicable Scales (pp 1190–1196)

The table on p **1194** applies only to distributions made between 9 March 1982 and 14 March 1983. For later distributions the table below may be used.

Distributions made after 14 March 1983 — grossing up at 20 per cent of full rate

Net cumulative total		*Reduced rate on slice per cent*	*Tax payable*		
£	£		£	£	£
60,000	— 79,400	3	Nil	+ 3/97 for each £ over	60,000
79,400	— 108,350	3.5	600	+ 7/193	79,400
108,350	— 137,150	4	1,650	+ 1/24	108,350
137,150	— 170,575	4.5	2,850	+ 9/191	137,150
170,575	— 213,325	5	4,425	+ 1/19	170,575
213,325	— 260,325	6	6,675	+ 3/47	213,325
260,325	— 660,225	7	9,675	+ 7/93	260,325
660,225	— 1,235,225	8	39,775	+ 2/23	660,225
1,235,225	— 2,440,975	9	89,775	+ 9/91	1,235,225
Over £2,440,975		10	209,025	+ 1/9	2,440,975

In *Stenhouse's Trustees* v *Lord Advocate* [1984] STC 195 trustees were empowered to divide a fund between three beneficiaries provided they had attained the age of 22. The trustees purported to divide the fund on 8 April 1975, when two beneficiaries had attained 22, but the third did not reach that age until 5 August 1977. It was held that the interests were severable, and that the appointments in favour of two beneficiaries were valid, but the third was *ultra vires*. Only the two valid appointments got the benefit of the 90 per cent reduction of tax under FA 1975, Sched 5, para 14.

Survivorship Clauses (pp 1226–1233)

The decision of Nourse J in the *Aird (No 1)* case at pp **1229–1231** was unanimously reversed by the Court of Appeal at [1983] STC 700. The court agreed with the Revenue's contention that the contingency on which the interests of the settlor's two children vested was not their surviving another person by a period of one day.

There was a preliminary question which Nourse J had not

thought necessary to answer. Does surviving another person by one day involve surviving for 24 hours precisely calculated from the time of the event (the *punctum temporis* construction) or does it involve surviving for 24 hours from the end of the day on which the event occurs (the 'day excluded' construction)? After considering such cases as *Lester* v *Garland* (1808) 15 Ves 248 (cited at p 722 of the First Edition of this book) the Court held that the *prima facie* presumption was in favour of the 'day excluded' construction, and that in the *Aird* case there was nothing to displace that presumption. Considerations of convenience and certainty strongly favoured it, because it is frequently not possible to establish the precise moment of death, and where the decedent is selected by a random process his relatives may not take kindly to impertinent inquiries from complete strangers. Accordingly, what the appointment required was that Sir John Aird should survive until midnight on Sunday 30 November 1975.

Could it then be genuinely said that it was Sir John's surviving another person (Major Bisgood) that caused his interest to vest? Oliver LJ said it was certain that someone, somewhere, would die on Saturday 29 November. Looking at the matter on the previous day when the appointment was executed, there were the following uncertainties:

(1) Sir John might fail to survive until Monday morning, in which event the interest would fail.

(2) Sir John might survive and Monday's *Times* might carry no announcement of a death on Saturday. In that event the interest would fail. (One can ignore for the purpose of analysis the fall-back on the *Daily Telegraph*, where exactly the same considerations apply.)

(3) Sir John might survive but there might be no *Times* on Monday. In that event it would not be known whether the interest would vest or fail until the next edition was published and it could be seen whether it contained the name of a person who died on Saturday.

(4) Sir John might survive and Monday's *Times* might be published and carry the announcement of the death of a person who died on the previous Saturday. In this event the interest would vest.

In each case the vesting of the interest was contingent upon Sir John's surviving to Sunday night, but the event in each case which actually caused the interest to vest or fail would not be the death of another person on Saturday plus survival till Monday morning but the publication of *The Times*, whenever that took place. The Court therefore concluded that there was no genuine contingency of surviving another person until Monday morning within the terms of para 6(7) of Sched 5 to the Finance Act 1975.

The Newspaper-Franco device was extensively used, and no doubt in some cases the period of survival was measured in hours rather than days. It seems unlikely that that circumstance would have persuaded the Court of Appeal to a different decision. The presumption against the '*punctum temporis*' construction might be slightly less strong, but it is thought that the 'day excluded' construction would still have prevailed. Oliver LJ said that the period of one day meant and could only mean 24 hours; so he evidently made no distinction between the two terms. He added: 'One has to approach the document on the footing that it might become material to inquire whether or not the contingency expressed has occurred, and it seems to me therefore that everything points to the likelihood that those who framed the appointment would intend a meaning which was ascertainable with complete certainty and without the necessity of making any embarrassing outside inquiry'. That would apply as much to a period expressed in hours as to one expressed in days. Waller LJ said that the difficulties of adopting a construction of 24 hours from the point of time of death would be almost insuperable; and presumably he too would have held that the period of 24 hours (or any other number of hours) must run from midnight on the day of death.

The effect of the decision on other variants of the Franco device remains to be evaluated. As noted at pp **1230–1231**, the Revenue have admitted that the device gives exemption where beneficial entitlement was effectively contingent on surviving the death before 7 April 1976 of a named individual, or of the first to die of a relatively small class, such as Members of Parliament. Other variants might require the beneficiary to survive the first to die of a much larger class, such as the persons named in *Who's Who*, or might rely on selection of a decedent by a random process involving, for instance, hospitals or coroners' courts. In all of them the relevant question is whether survival of another person for the requisite period is genuinely the contingency upon which in the event the interest depends. As Oliver LJ said, it is no use dressing up your trusts so as to make it appear that the contingency is survival of another person when in fact it is something else.

TRANSITIONAL PROVISIONS

Subsections (3) and (4) of FA 1976, s 105 (p **1232**), ceased to have effect on 26 July 1984: FA 1984, Sched 21, para 21. They related to deaths before 1977 and had long been obsolescent.

Temporary Charitable Trusts (pp 1240–1242)

Section 102 of the Finance Act 1984 inserts a new subs (6A) into s 113 of the Finance Act 1982, which relates to the tapered charge of tax on property leaving a temporary charitable trust. Under the new subsection, where the tax charge is attributable wholly or partly to property which was excluded property throughout, or at any time during, the relevant period (as defined in subs (7)) no quarter throughout which that property was excluded property will be counted in calculating the rate of tax. This takes effect from 9 March 1982, ie, it is retrospective to the beginning of the new discretionary trust regime.

The new subs (6A) applies also to the tapered charges on property leaving accumulation and maintenance trusts (p **1252**), employee trusts (p **1260**), newspaper trusts (p **1262**), protective trusts (p **1267**) and trusts for disabled persons (p **1269**).

Accumulation and Maintenance Trusts (1242–1255)

THE FIRST CONDITION

The decision in *Inglewood* v *IRC* [1981] STC 318 (not 91, as misprinted at p **1244**) was upheld by the Court of Appeal at [1983] STC 133. The question was whether the words 'will . . . become entitled' in para 15(1) (*a*) of Sched 5 to the Finance Act 1975 imported some degree of certainty or whether, as the trustees argued, they should be interpreted *rebus sic stantibus*, that is, unless something happens to frustrate the contingent entitlement. Vinelott J had described the trustees' construction as an impossible one. The Court of Appeal did not go as far as that, because in *Green* v *Bowes-Lyon* [1963] AC 420 the House of Lords held that in deciding whether a tenancy 'will not come to an end within 14 months or less' you must simply have regard to the question at the relevant date and not to all the future possibilities. But in *Green's* case the decision was much influenced by the context of the statute, which contained a strong indication against futurity. In *Inglewood* the context of para 15 supported the Revenue view.

The trustees argued that it did not make sense to treat 'will' as meaning 'will inevitably', because—

(*a*) a beneficiary may lawfully dispose of his interest after he attains 18 and before it vests in possession,
(*b*) his interest may be taken away from him on bankruptcy,
(*c*) his interest may be prevented from vesting in him by an order of court, eg, under the Variation of Trusts Act 1958, or
(*d*) he may die before attaining a vested interest.

The Court found no substance in point (*d*). Paragraph 15 was dealing with contingent interests. A trust could not be excluded from the operation of the paragraph because of the possible happening of an event inherent in the contingency which brought the trust within the paragraph in the first place.

The answer to points (*a*), (*b*) and (*c*) was that para 15 began with the words 'This paragraph applies to any settlement where . . .'. The Court construed 'where' as meaning 'whereby' and held that para 15 was concerned only with provisions contained in the settlement itself. None of the matters in (*a*), (*b*) and (*c*) could be so described.

More importantly the trustees contended that, if the Revenue were right, any trust which did not exclude the power of advancement in s 32 of the Trustee Act 1925 would be outside para 15. The statutory power must be exercised only for the benefit of the person contingently entitled, but the word 'benefit' has been very widely construed, so that the primary beneficiaries might be the children of that person, as in *Re Hampden* [1977] TR 177, or charities, as in *Re Clore* [1966] 1 WLR 955. The trustees argued that this power was in substance no different from a power of revocation. But the Court thought there was a vital difference: the purpose of a power of advancement is to aid the beneficial trusts and not to destroy them. It would be artificial to regard such a power as taking the trust out of para 15. The statutory power of advancement is so commonly incorporated in trusts that para 15(1)(*a*) must be read so as to accommodate it and not to withdraw the relief from a trust containing such a power.

It may be observed that the language of s 114(1)(*a*) of the Finance Act 1982 is a little different from that of para 15(1)(*a*). 'This paragraph applies to any settlement where . . .' is replaced by 'this section applies to settled property if. . .'. It is not so easy to infer from the new wording that the conditions following the word 'if' must depend solely on the terms of the settlement. However, the official view is that s 114(1)(*a*) was not intended to change, and did not change, the law in this respect. It is thought that 'will' still imports a degree of certainty. There is much weight in the Court's conclusion that it seems 'highly unlikely that the benefit of para 15 was intended to be available to what were, in effect, discretionary trusts . . . merely by the device of a primary trust for a person at 25 which could be revoked at any time'.

THE PROTECTIVE TRUSTS TRAP

The decision of Nourse J in *Egerton* v *IRC* at [1982] STC 520 was unheld by the Court of Appeal at [1983] STC 531, [1983] TCA 450. As noted at p **1255**, the question was one of construction of s 71(2) of the Finance Act 1978, which begins by providing that the section shall be deemed to have come into force on 11 April 1978 and ends with the words 'by reason only of the coming into force of this section'. The taxpayers contended that the words quoted must refer to the actual coming into force of the section (ie, at the date of the Royal Assent) and not the deemed coming into force. The Court of Appeal rejected this construction because—

(1) The last part of s 71(2) is separated from the first part only by a semi-colon. It is not permissible to read the phrase 'the coming into force of this section' as referring to its actual coming into force, when the draftsman has provided his own dictionary by stating that the whole section shall be deemed to have come into force on another date.

(2) Section 71(2) refers to the coming into force of 'this section' rather than 'this Act', lending strength to the conclusion that it was intended to refer to something other than the coming into force of the Act itself.

(3) The words 'but' and 'only' in s 71(2) support the argument of the Crown. Reading the section (as one must) on the footing that it came into force on 11 April 1978, one finds that the charge arises not only by reason of the coming into force of the section but by the joint effect of such coming into force and the execution of an appointment by the trustees on 19 July 1978.

(4) There is no obvious legislative purpose that would have been achieved by granting an amnesty to trusts which fell into the 'protective trusts trap' (deliberately or otherwise) between 11 April 1978 and 31 July 1978.

The taxpayers therefore failed in their attempt to join the 'club' of accumulation and maintenance trusts without paying the membership fee.

Employee Trusts (pp 1255–1262)

FA 1975, Sched 5, para 17(3)(*b*) (p **1258**) now requires a small interest in possession to be disregarded for the purposes of 'this Part of this Act (except subsection (3) of section 23 and section 20(4) so far as relating to that subsection)': FA 1984, Sched 21, para 12. This amendment is evidently to facilitate consolidation and seems to have no significant consequences. The exception forestalls possible tax avoidance where a beneficiary in possession buys the reversionary interest.

Newspaper Trusts (p 1262)

The last sentence on the page appears to be wrong. The difference between the side-notes to ss 115 and 116 of the Finance Act 1982 suggests that s 115 was not intended to apply to newspaper trusts, and this may be a case where the courts would pay some attention to the side-note (*see* Lord Upjohn's remarks cited at pp 3–4, above). More importantly, s 115 speaks of property 'held on trusts of the description specified in paragraph 17(1) of Schedule 5 to the Finance Act 1975', while s 116 in contrast speaks of 'property to which paragraph 17 . . . applies'. The words last cited clearly cover newspaper trusts, but the words first cited probably do not. In any case it is unlikely that a newspaper trust would satisfy all the conditions in s 115(2).

Trusts for Disabled Persons (pp 1267–1271)

The reference at p **1268** to the Mental Health Act 1959 should now be read as one to the Mental Health Act 1983.

Capital Transfer Tax Forms (pp 1273–1274)

England and Wales

The layout of Cap Form 202 has been revised and its scope extended. The new version of the form is reproduced at pp 60–63, below. It is to be used where the total net value of the estate, after deducting any exemptions and reliefs claimed, does not exceed the threshold above which capital transfer tax is payable at the date of death and both (*a*) the deceased died on or after 27 March 1981 domiciled in the United Kingdom; and

(*b*) the estate comprises only property which has passed under the deceased's will or intestacy or by nomination or beneficially by survivorship; and all that property was situate in the United Kingdom.

In all other estates form 200 (UK domicile) or 201 (overseas domicile) should be used, *unless* the estate is an excepted estate under the CTT (Delivery of Account) Regulations in which case no account need be completed, although exceptionally one may be required later.

The layout of two other forms — Cap C5 and Cap 30 — has also been revised, following consultations with the Law Society and the Consultative Committee of Accountancy Bodies. Both forms were introduced on 1 August 1984 and are reproduced at pp 64-69, below.

Northern Ireland

A form similar to the new English form 202 was introduced in March 1984.

Scotland

The Cap Form B-4 is the nearest equivalent to the form 202. Because of the new regulations (SI 1983 No 1040) mentioned at p 24, above, and printed at p 93, below, the limit of £25,000 at p **1273** is increased to £40,000.

The Scottish inventory forms are being redesigned, and it is hoped that the new ones will be available early in 1985 with corresponding instructions.

Inland Revenue
Capital Transfer Tax

For Official Use		
A		
Date of Grant		
Index	Reader	Stats

Inland Revenue Account

For use for an original full grant where

- **the deceased died on or after 27 March 1981 domiciled in the United Kingdom;**
- **the estate comprises only property which has passed under the deceased's Will or Intestacy or by nomination or beneficially by survivorship, and all that property was situate in the United Kingdom; and**
- **the total net value of the estate, after deducting any Exemptions and Reliefs claimed, does not exceed the threshhold above which Capital Transfer Tax is payable at the date of death.**

In all other cases form Cap 200 or 201 as appropriate must be used, unless the estate is an excepted estate under the CTT (Delivery Of Accounts) Regulations. For an excepted estate no account need be completed, although exceptionally one may be required later.

Name and address of person to whom any communication should be sent .... Reference ....

.... Telephone No. ....

....

Post town .... Postcode ....

(a) Insert "Principal" or "District" as required, and in the latter case add the name of the district.

In the High Court of Justice Family Division (Probate)

The (a) Registry

In the estate of (please use CAPITAL letters)

Surname			
Title and Forenames *(in full)*			
Date of Birth		**Date of Death**	
Last usual address		**Marital Status**	*tick "✓" as appropriate* **married** ☐ **divorced** ☐ **single** ☐ **widowed** ☐
		Surviving Relatives	*tick "✓" as appropriate* **Husband** ☐ **Child(ren)** ☐ **Wife** ☐ **Parent(s)** ☐
	Postcode	**Occupation**	
Country of Domicile *(tick "✓" as appropriate)* **England and Wales** ☐ **Scotland** ☐ **N. Ireland** ☐			

Names and addresses of executors or intending administrators:

Postcode	**Postcode**
Postcode	**Postcode**

Cap 202

Declaration

(b) Insert kind of grant

1. I/We desire to obtain a grant of (b)

2. To the best of my/our knowledge and belief all the statements and particulars furnished in this account and its accompanying schedules are true and complete.

No alteration is permitted to paragraphs 2, 3, 4, 5, 6 and 7

3. The deceased made no transfers of value chargeable with Capital Transfer Tax (ie no transfers of value that were not covered by the CTT exemptions) after 26 March 1974 and within 10 years of the death.

4. Account "A" is a complete and true account of all the property comprised in the estate at the death in respect of which the grant is to be made and of its value at that time.

5. Account "B" is a complete and true account of any nominated property, and of any property held jointly with any other person(s) the beneficial interest in which passed by survivorship, and of its value at the date of death.

6. No property situate outside the United Kingdom was comprised in the estate at the death.

7. The deceased did not have an interest in settled property at his death nor had he after 26 March 1974 and within 10 years of his death an interest in settled property or settled any property.

Signed by the above-named	Signed by the above-named
date	date
Signed by the above-named	Signed by the above-named
date	date

Warning: An executor or intending administrator who fails to make full enquiries and personally verify that the statements in this account are true may make himself liable to prosecution or penalties.

Account A – property of the deceased in respect of which the grant is to be made

Property without the instalment option	Gross value at date of death (before deduction of exemption(s) or relief(s))
	£
1. British Savings Bonds and other Government Securities, Savings Certificates and Premium Bonds. (Give description and state amount of each security held, attaching a schedule if necessary.) In the case of Savings Certificates please attach a letter from the Savings Certificates Division or a list giving details of purchase and value of each certificate at date of death.	
2. Other Stocks, Shares or Investments including Unit Trusts. (Give details on form Cap 40 or similar schedule attached and state in adjoining column total value of all investments.)	
3. Cash and Cash at Bank, Savings Banks or in Building, Co-operative or Friendly Societies, including interest to date of death (state each separately and attach a schedule if necessary).	
4. Policies of Insurance a. on the life of the deceased, including any bonuses thereon (state each item separately, giving names of companies). b. on the life of any other person (enter surrender value and attach letter from the Company).	

5. Household and Personal Goods (furniture, jewellery, clothes, car, etc).

6. Other Assets not included above or as instalment option property opposite. (If space is insufficient please give details on schedule attached and state in adjoining column total value of these assets.)

Total 1

Debts due from the deceased	Amount
1. Debts (other than mortgage and business debts) Name and address of creditor | Description of debt (If there is insufficient space to list all debts a schedule should be attached.) 2. Funeral expenses (cost of tombstone must not be included).	£
Total 2	

Instalment option property	Gross value at date of death (before deduction of exemption(s) or relief(s))
1. Freehold and leasehold property (form Cap 37B should also be completed) situated at .... 2. Business interests (state nature of business ....) a. Net value of deceased's interest in business, as statement or balance sheet annexed. b. Net value of deceased's interest as a partner in the firm of .... as statement annexed.	£
Total 3	

Debts due in respect of instalment option property	Amount
1. Mortgages on freehold and leasehold property (amount outstanding at date of death) Date of mortgage .... Property on which mortgage charged .... To whom owed .... 2. Other debts (If space is insufficient please attach a schedule) Name and address of creditor | Description of debt	£
Total 4	

3

Joint Property – Questions

	Tick "✓" as appropriate
Was the deceased joint owner of any property of any description or did he hold any money on a joint account (apart from property or money of which he was merely a trustee)?	**Yes** ☐ **No** ☐
If so, please give full particulars including a. the date when the joint ownership began (or the date of opening the joint account) b. the name(s) of the other owner(s) c. by whom and from what source the joint property was provided and, if it or its purchase price was contributed by one or more of the joint owners, the extent of the contribution made by each d. how the income (if any) was dealt with and enjoyed e. what is considered to be the extent of the deceased's share or interest	

Account B – Nominated and joint property

	Gross value at date of death (before deduction of exemption(s) and relief(s)
	£
Full description of property, real and personal, being nominated property and property held jointly with any other person(s) the beneficial interest in which passed by survivorship. (Show gross value at date of death of the proportion chargeable to tax. If space is insufficient, please attach a schedule.) Total 5	
Less appropriate share of debts or incumbrances thereon. (Give details. If space is insufficient, please attach a schedule.)	
Total 6	
Value for probate purposes	£
Gross estate **per total 1** **per total 3** ______ Total 7	
Less debts **per total 2** **per total 4** ______	
Net estate for probate purposes Total 8	
Value of estate for tax purposes	£
Nominated and joint property (net) as total 6	
Net estate for Probate purposes as total 8	
Total 9	
Deduct Exemptions and Reliefs claimed 1. Agricultural relief : Schedule annexed 2. Business relief : Schedule annexed 3. Spouse exemption : Schedule annexed 4. Other (please specify)	
Net estate for tax purposes	

Prints of this form can be obtained from the Capital Taxes Office, Inland Revenue, Rockley Road, London, W14 0DF, and on personal application only at the Stamps Office, Room 2, South West Wing, Bush House, Strand, WC2B 4QN, the London Chief Post Office, King Edward Street, EC1A 1AA, the Branch Post Offices at Fleet Street, EC4Y 1BT, Chancery Lane, WC2A 1EA, East Strand, WC2R 1EL, High Holborn, WC1V 6RN, 11 Regent Street, SW1 and Throgmorton Avenue (57 London Wall, EC2) and Main Post Offices in England and Wales outside the Metropolitan Postal District

4829L D8393232 P1 Gp 3648

CTO Reference

Inland Revenue
Capital Transfer Tax

Account of a Transfer of Value

- Please read the notes in Cap 210 before completing this account. The references in this account to *"notes"* are to notes in Cap 210.
- You do not need to deliver an account for every transfer. *See page 1, Cap 210.*
- Please send the completed account to the Capital Taxes Office, Rockley Road, London W14 0DF; or to the Capital Taxes Office, 16 Picardy Place, Edinburgh EH1 3NB; or to the Capital Taxes Office, Law Courts Building, Chichester Street, Belfast BT1 3NU, as appropriate.

1. Name and address of person to whom any communication should be sent .... Reference ....

.... Telephone No. ....

....

Post town ....

County .... Postcode ....

2. Date of Transfer *see note 2* ....

3. Transferor (If the transfer is the disposal or termination of an interest in possession in settled property this means the person entitled to that interest, not the settlor or trustee(s) *see note 3)*

Surname *CAPITAL letters*			
Title and first names *in full*			
Date of birth		and, if dead, date of death	
Usual (or last usual) address	Postcode	Marital status	
		Place of domicile	

4. Transferee(s) *see note 4*

- If the transfer is the termination of an interest in possession in settled property and any person now entitled to the property has died please state the date and the official reference to his/her estate if known
- Attach a schedule if there are more than 3 transferees or if space is insufficient

Full name(s) and address(es)	Relationship (if any) to transferor	Interest taken
Postcode		
Postcode		
Postcode		

Cap C 5

5A. The Transfer *see note 5A* *Tick "✓" and complete as appropriate.*

1. Was the transfer associated in any way with any formal or informal settlement or trust or joint interest, or with any deed or will?	☐ Yes, (copies of the relevant deeds are attached/have already been produced (under official reference .... (*or* ((in the case of a will) the full name and date of death of the testator (are given in the attached schedule. ☐ No
2. Was the transfer of, or in any way related to the purchase of, or other dealing with, a policy of assurance or an annuity?	☐ Yes, copies of the relevant policies, etc, are attached. ☐ No
3. Was the transfer associated with any (other) change in, or release of, rights, or merger of interest - e.g. in, or in the shares of, a limited company?	☐ Yes, details are given in the attached schedule ☐ No
4. Was a close company involved in the transfer?	☐ Yes, full details (including the company's name, registered office and company registration number) are given in the attached schedule. ☐ No
5. Is the transfer connected in any way with any other transfer — past, in prospect, or taking effect at the same time?	☐ Yes, (already disclosed under official reference .... (*or* (full details are given in the attached schedule. ☐ No
6. Transfers of land Did the transferor or spouse retain land adjacent to that now transferred?	☐ Yes, full details of the retained land and estimated values before and after this transfer are given in the attached schedule. ☐ No ☐ Not applicable
7. Transfer of shares in a private company a. Did the transferor or spouse immediately before the transfer hold other shares or securities in the company?	☐ Yes, details are given in the attached schedule. ☐ No ☐ Not applicable
b. Did the transferor at any time after 26 March 1974 and within 10 years of the transfer have control of the company?	☐ Yes, details are given in the attached schedule. ☐ No ☐ Not applicable

Date of Transfer	**5B Details of Transfer** *see note 5B* *Attach schedules if necessary*	Price or basis of valuation	Value £	For Official Use
		Total		
	5C Deductions *see note 5C* *Attach schedules if necessary*	Amount £		
		Total		
	Net value disregarding any capital transfer tax on the transfer, reliefs and exemptions			
	5D Reliefs and Exemptions Claimed *see note 5D* *Complete as applicable and give details*	Amount £		
	Reliefs			
	1. Agricultural			
	2. Business			
	3. Other (specify)			
	Exemptions			
	1. Annual (year of transfer (previous year			
	2. Other (specify)			
		Total		
	Total less deductions, reliefs and exemptions			

6 Payment of tax *see note 6* *Tick "✓" and complete as appropriate*

1. Is the tax chargeable on this transfer to be borne by the transferor?	☐ Yes ☐ No, the tax will be paid from the following source
2. If you are entitled to pay any of the tax by instalments, do you elect to do so?	on the following items: – ☐ Yes, yearly ☐ Yes, half yearly (transfers before 15 March 1983 only) ☐ No ☐ Not applicable
3. Are any deductions against tax claimed?	☐ Yes, as follows:- ☐ No

7 Other Transfers *see note 7*

Have any other transfers of value (other than those wholly exempt) been made by this transferor since 26 March 1974?	☐ Yes, details already disclosed under official reference *or* full details of the other transfer(s) (including copies of any relevant deeds etc) together with the transferor's full name and address at that time are given in the attached schedule. ☐ No

8 Declaration by the transferor or other person(s) required to deliver this account *see note 8*

If the transfer involves settled property the declaration should be completed by all the trustees but it may avoid further enquiries in such cases if the life tenant (below) /liferent(er)(rix), if living, were to join in the declaration.

To the best of my/our knowledge and belief the statements and particulars furnished in this account and the accompanying schedules are true and complete *(agents must not sign this declaration).*

Full name and address	Signature and capacity	date
Postcode		
Postcode		
Postcode		
Postcode		

Warning.— if you fail to verify personally that the statements in this account are true and complete you may make yourself liable to prosecution or penalties.

Print of this form and of the instructions (Cap 210) can be obtained from the Capital Taxes Office, at any of the addresses shown on page 1 of this account, and on personal application only at the Stamps Office, Room 2, South West Wing, Bush House, Strand WC2, the London Chief Post Office, King Edward Street EC1, the Branch Post Office at Fleet Street EC4, Chancery Lane WC2, East Strand WC2, High Holborn WC1, 11 Regent Street SW1, and Throgmorton Avenue EC2, and Main Post Offices in England and Wales outside the Metropolitan Postal District.

PRINTED IN THE UK FOR HMSO. Dd. 8393165. 3/84. 44577.

Inland Revenue
Capital Transfer Tax/Estate Duty

CTO reference

Application for a certificate under
Finance Act 1975 Sched 4 Para 25(2) or
Finance Act 1894 S 11 (2)

Your reference:

Telephone No:

Name and address of the person to whom the certificate is to be sent

- **Do not submit this form until you believe that no adjustment of the amount of tax or duty paid will be necessary.**
- **Complete section A or B or C (as appropriate) and sections D, E and F.**
- **Only trustees may normally apply for a certificate in respect of a lifetime transfer.**
- **If space is insufficient attach a schedule.**
- **The completed form should be sent in duplicate to the Capital Taxes Office, Rockley Road, London W14 0DF or Law Courts Building, Chichester Street, Belfast BT1 3NU, according to where the original papers were submitted.**

A Liability arising on death

Full name of deceased:

Date of death:

Title:

Beneficiaries entitled to the assets *(Describe in general terms but give the status of any by reference to whom any exemption or relief is claimed):*

B Liability in respect of a lifetime transfer

Full name of transferor (ie in the case of settled property the person entitled to the interest in possession):

Date of birth:

Date of transfer:

Details of that transfer:

C Liability in respect of a settlement without an interest in possession

Full title and date of settlement:

Date of chargeable event:

Details of that event:

Cap 30

S5973 (26201) Dd.8393160 50m 5/84 G.W.B.Ltd. Gp.870

D The property or value transferred in respect of which this application is made is included in the
(complete or delete as appropriate)

Account(s)/Affidavit(s) dated ....
Corrective Account(s)/Affidavit(s) dated ....
Corrective Assessment(s) dated ....
Letter(s) dated ....

Tick "✓" as appropriate

Have any additions or amendments come to light since the above were submitted? ☐ **Yes** ☐ **No**

- **If *YES* give details:**

E Except as mentioned at D above

is there any other property passing or taxable on the death *or* ☐ **Yes** ☐ **No**

have there been any previous chargeable transfers *or* ☐ **Yes** ☐ **No**

have there been any previous events on which tax was chargeable or which may affect the amount of tax chargeable? ☐ **Yes** ☐ **No**

- **If *YES* give details:**

F Declaration

To the best of my/our knowledge and belief the information given is correct.
I/We am/are not aware of any other information which should be disclosed.
I/We apply for a statutory certificate of discharge.

Signed:	Signed:
Date:	Date:
Name:	Name:
Capacity:	Capacity:
Signed:	Signed:
Date:	Date:
Name:	Name:
Capacity:	Capacity:

Certificate

The Commissioners of Inland Revenue discharge the above-named applicants from any (further) claim for tax or duty on the value attributable to the property specified at D on the occasion specified at A/B/C

Signed: Date:

For and on behalf of the Commissioners

- If no duty or tax has been paid this certificate does not constitute a determination of the values of individual items for any Revenue purpose. In particular values are not "ascertained" for Capital Gains Tax within the meaning of s 26 of the Finance Act 1965 and s 153 and Sched 6 Para 9 Capital Gains Tax Act 1979.
- A certificate is not valid in certain circumstances, such as in the case of fraud or failure to disclose material facts or where further tax becomes payable as a result of an instrument of variation – see Sched 4 Para 25(4) Finance Act 1975.

Prints of this form can be obtained from the Capital Taxes Office at either of the addresses overleaf and on personal application only at the Stamps Office, Room 2, South West Wing, Bush House, Strand WC2, the London Chief Post Office, King Edward Street EC1, the Branch Post Offices at Fleet Street EC4, Chancery Lane WC2, High Holborn WC1, Regent Street SW1 and Throgmorton Avenue EC2 and Main Post Offices in England and Wales outside the Metropolitan Postal District.

PART 2: STATUTES, ETC

Amendments to Vol 2

In these amendments '1975' stands for the Finance Act 1975, and so on for subsequent years.

p **19** 1975, s 22(4). Amended by 1984, Sched 21, para 1. The revised wording is printed at p 46–47 above.

p **24** 1975, s 25(10). The words '(except subsection (8))' are inserted after the word 'section' by 1984, Sched 21, para 2.

pp **24–25** 1975, s 26(2). Two amendments (described at p 20 above) are made by 1984, Sched 21, para 3, with effect from 26 July 1984.

p **25** 1975, s 26(3). The words '10(1)(*b*) or', 'given to a charity or property' and 'charity or, as the case may be, the' are repealed by F(2)A 1983, Sched 2, Pt II, with effect from 15 March 1983.

p **27** 1975, s 28(1). New subsections (1) and (1A) are substituted by F(2)A 1983, s 13(1), with effect from 26 July 1983.

p **28** 1975, s 28(8). A new subs (8) is substituted by F(2)A 1983, s 13(2), with effect from 26 July 1983.

p **35** 1975, s 37. In subs (1)(*b*) the word 'previous' is inserted before 'chargeable transfers' by 1983, Sched 9, para 3. New tables are substituted in subs (3) by F(2)A 1983, s 8(2), with effect from 15 March 1983, and by 1984, s 101(2), with effect from 13 March 1984.

pp **43–44** 1975, s 45. After the words 'as domiciled in the United Kingdom' in subs (1), the words '(and not elsewhere)' are inserted by 1984, Sched 21, para 4, with effect from 26 July 1984. Subsection (1)(*c*) ceased to have effect on 15 March 1983 and has been repealed: F(2)A 1983, s 12(1) and Sched 2, Pt II. Subsections (2A) and (3) are repealed with effect from the same date.

p **46** 1975, s 47. A new subs (1AA) (*see* pp 8–9 above) is inserted by 1984, s 103(1), in relation to deaths after 12 March 1984.

p **48** 1975, s 51(1). The words '"charity" and "charitable" have the same meanings as in the Income Tax Acts' were omitted in error. The definition of 'enactment' has ceased to have effect: 1984, Sched 21, para 5(*a*). A new definition of 'land' (printed at p 25 above) is inserted by 1984, Sched 21, para 5(*b*).

p **49** 1975, s 51(3). Repealed by 1984, Sched 21, para 4, and Sched 29, Pt IX, with effect from 26 July 1984.

p **52** 1975, Sched 4, para 2. The word 'relevant' in the last line but two of subpara (2A) is changed to 'appropriate' by 1983, Sched 9, para 4.

p **55** 1975, Sched 4, para 5(3). The word 'of' at the end of line 3 of para (*b*) should be 'or'.

p **56** 1975, Sched 4, para 6(6). Amended by 1984, Sched 21, para 6, as noted at p 27–28 above.

p **58** 1975, Sched 4, para 10(2). '£25' is substituted for '£1' by 1984, s 127 and Sched 22, para 6, with effect from a date to be fixed by statutory instrument.

p **59** 1975, Sched 4, para 11(2). '£20' has become level 1 on the standard scale: Criminal Justice Act 1982, ss 37, 38(1), (6) and (8), 46(1) and (4)(*a*) and 75.

p **59** 1975, Sched 4, para 12(3). The words 'a charity or only' are repealed with effect from 15 March 1983 by F(2)A 1983, Sched 2, Pt II.

pp **60–64** 1975, Sched 4, paras 13(1), 14(1) and 15. For the words 'at his option either by eight equal yearly instalments or by sixteen equal half-yearly instalments' the words 'ten equal yearly instalments' are substituted with effect from 15 March 1983 by F(2)A 1983, s 11(1). In para 13(3) '£20,000' is substituted for '£5,000' by s 11(2) with effect from the same date. In para 14(2) the word 'net' is inserted before 'value of an interest' by 1984, Sched 21, para 7.

p **68** 1975, Sched 4, para 19(2). The words 'a charity or only' are repealed by F(2)A 1983, Sched 2, Pt II, with effect from 15 March 1983.

p **69** 1975, Sched 4, para 19(4). The words 'to any person' and 'of that person' are repealed by 1984, Sched 21, para 8, and Sched 23, Pt IX.

p **71** 1975, Sched 4, para 22. New paras 22A and 22B are added by 1984, s 106(1), with effect from 26 July 1984 (*see* p 27 above).

p **72** 1975, Sched 4, para 23(3). Words substituted by 1984, s 105(1) (*see* p 26 above), with effect from 1 April 1983.

p **76** 1975, Sched 4, para 36. A new para 36A is added by 1984, s 106(2), with effect from 26 July 1984 (*see* p 27 above).

p **78** 1975, Sched 4, para 44. Repealed by 1984, Sched 21, para 9, and Sched 23, Pt IX.

p **80** 1975, Sched 5, para 1(8). For the words 'and section 25(3)(*d*) of this Act' 1984, Sched 21, para 10, substitutes 'sections 22(2) and (3), 24(3) and 25(3)(*d*) of this Act and sections 93 and 94' with effect from 26 July 1984.

p **84** 1975, Sched 5, para 4(7). After the words 'surviving spouse' 1984, Sched 21, para 11, inserts '(or surviving former spouse)'.

p **84** 1975, Sched 5, para 4(10). After the words 'in this paragraph' the words 'and in section 46(5)' are inserted by 1983, Sched 9, para 5.

p **97** 1975, Sched 5, para 17(3)(*b*). Amended as noted at p 58 above by 1984, Sched 21, para 12.

p **101** 1975, Sched 5, para 19(4)(*a*). The date '1983' is substituted for '1959' by the Mental Health Act 1983, Sched 4, para 40.

p **102** 1975, Sched 5, para 22. For the words 'this Schedule' 1984, Sched 21, para 13, substitutes 'this Part of this Act'.

p **104** 1975, Sched 5, para 24. Amended by 1984, Sched 21, para 14(2) and (3), as noted at p 9 above.

p **111** 1975, Sched 6, para 10(1). Paragraph (*b*) has ceased to have effect in relation to transfers of value made on or after 15 March 1983 and is repealed: F(2)A 1983, s 9(1) and Sched 2, Pt II.

p **113** 1975, Sched 6, para 12. 'The Historic Buildings and Monuments Commission for England' is inserted immediately before 'The National Trust for Places of Historic Interest or Natural Beauty' by 1983, s 46(5), with effect from 13 May 1983.

p **124** 1975, Sched 7 para 1. The words 'was employed as mentioned in subpara (3) below or' and 'and not being so employed' in subpara (2) and the whole of subpara (3) were repealed by the Armed Forces Act 1981, Sched 5.

pp **125–126** 1975, Sched 7, para 3(2A). A new para 3(2AA) is inserted by 1984, s 104(2), with effect from 15 March 1983.

pp **126–127** 1975, Sched 7, para 4(2)(*b*). Amended by 1984, Sched 21, para 15, as noted at p 31 above.

p **128** 1975, Sched 7, para 6(1). The words 'citizen of the United Kingdom and colonies' are replaced by 'British citizen, a British Dependent Territories citizen or a British Overseas citizen' with effect from 1 January 1983: British Nationality Act 1981, s 51(3).

p **142** 1975, Sched 10, para 1(1). Words 'a person's estate' are substituted for 'a transferor's estate' by 1984, Sched 21, para 16.

p **143** 1975, Sched 10, para 5(1)(*b*). The word 'for' is substituted for 'by' by 1984, Sched 21, para 17.

p **145** 1975, Sched 10, para 9(1). Clauses added by 1984, s 96(8) and Sched 9, para 14, as follows:

'(*e*) allowance should be made for a liability for income tax in respect of an offshore income gain, within the meaning of Chapter VII of Part II of the Finance Act 1984, arising on a disposal which is deemed to occur on the death by virtue of section 92(3) of that Act; and

(*f*) allowance shall be made for any liability to income tax arising under paragraph 1 of Schedule 9 to the Finance Act 1984 (cheap discount securities) on a disposal which is deemed to occur by virtue of paragraph 2(2) of that Schedule.'

p **149** 1975, Sched 10, para 12. Subpara (2) added by 1984, s 107(2) (*see* p 15 above) with effect from 10 March 1981.

p **163** 1975, Sched 10, para 40(4). 'Schedule 3 to the Town and Country Planning Act 1968' is replaced by 'the Compulsory Purchase (Vesting Declarations) Act 1981' under para 2 of Sched 3 to the latter Act.

p **169** 1976, s 76(3)(*b*). The words from 'or the value' to the end are repealed by 1984, Sched 21, para 20, and Sched 23, Pt IX.

p **172** 1976, s 78(4)(*b*). The words 'to the Board' and from 'or' to 'tax' are repealed by 1983, Sched 9, para 6.

p **197** 1976, s 105(3) and (4). Repealed by 1984, Sched 21, para 21, and Sched 23, Pt IX.

pp **200–201** 1976, s 114(6). The words 'the said section 37' are replaced by 'section 37 of the said Act of 1975' by 1983, Sched 9, para 7.

p **201** 1976, s 114(8). Repealed by 1984, s 105(2) and Sched 23, Pt IX, with effect from 1 April 1983.

p **203** 1976, s 117(5). The words 'Paragraphs 10 and 11 (gifts to charities and' are replaced by 'Paragraph 11 (gifts', and the words from 'those paragraphs' to '13 (gifts' are replaced by 'that paragraph and paragraphs 10, 12 and 13 (gifts to charities,' in relation to transfers of value made on or after 15 March 1983: F(2)A 1983, s 9(2).

p **209** 1976, s 123(2). The words '(which shall not constitute income for any tax purpose)' are inserted after 'shall carry interest' by 1984, Sched 21, para 22.

p **212** 1976, Sched 10, para 2(1A). Paragraph (*b*) ceased to have effect on 15 March 1983 and has been repealed, and in para (*c*) the letters ((*bb*) have been inserted after '3(1)' with effect from that date: F(2)A 1983, s 10(1) and Sched 2, Pt II.

p **219** 1976, Sched 11, para 2. Repealed by 1984, Sched 23, Pt IX, with effect from 26 July 1984.

pp **232–233** 1977, s 49. Repealed by F(2)A 1983, Sched 2, Pt II, with effect from 15 March 1983.

pp **271–274** 1980, Sched 15. 1984, Sched 21, para 23, substitutes 'other' for 'previous' in paras 2A, 5 and 6, and inserts '(or by the most recent of those reductions)' after 'by that reduction' in paras 5 and 6.

pp **283–284** 1981, s 97. A new subs (2) is substituted by 1984, s 107(3), with effect from 10 March 1981 (*see* p 6 above).

p **289** 1981, Sched 14, para 1(2). The meaning of 'farm buildings' is extended by 1984, s 107(1), with effect from 10 March 1981 (*see* p 16 above).

p **290** 1981, Sched 14, para 2. The figure '20' in sub-paras (2) and (4) has been increased to '30' by F(2)A 1983, s 10(2), with effect from 15 March 1983.

pp **291–294** 1981, Sched 14, paras 3, 4, 7, 8 and 11. The meaning of 'agriculture' is extended by 1984, s 107(1), with effect from 10 March 1981 (*see* p 16 above).

p **304** 1982, s 92(2). Repealed by F(2)A 1983, Sched 2, Pt II, with effect from 15 March 1983.

p **307** 1982, s 94(6). The words from 'and, in' to the end are repealed by 1984, Sched 21, para 24, and Sched 23, Pt IX.

p **311** 1982, s 103(3). The date '1981' at the foot of the page became '1982' on 28 January 1983: Insurance Companies Act 1982, Sched 5, para 28(*a*).

p **320** 1982, s 113. A new subs (6A) (*see* p 55 above) is inserted by 1984, s 102(1), in relation to events after 8 March 1982, and will accordingly be applied by 1982, ss 114, 116 and 118. In s 113(7) the words 'subsections (6) and (6A)' are substituted for 'subsection (6)' by 1984, s 102(2).

pp **326-328** 1982, ss 120 to 124. Amended by 1984, Sched 21, paras 25 and 26, as noted at p 47 and 50 above, with effect from 26 July 1984. The word 'house' in the first line of s 120 should be 'spouse'. A new subs (3) (*see* p 50 above) is added to s 121 by 1984, s 104(1), in relation to events after 14 March 1983.

pp **343-346** 1982, Sched 17, paras 9, 18 and 28. Repealed by 1984, Sched 23, Pt IX, with effect from 26 July 1984.

FINANCE ACT 1983

An Act to grant certain duties, to alter other duties and to amend the law relating to the National Debt and the Public Revenue, and to make further provision in connection with Finance.

[13 May 1983].

* * * * *

SCHEDULE 9

VALUE ADDED TAX, CAR TAX AND CAPITAL TRANSFER TAX CONSOLIDATION AMENDMENTS

* * * * *

Capital transfer tax

3 In Section 37 (1)(*b*) of the Finance Act 1975, after the words "transferred by" there shall be inserted the word "previous".

4 In paragraph 2 (2A) of Schedule 4 to that Act, for the words "relevant property" there shall be substituted the words "appropriate property".

5 In paragraph 4 (10) of Schedule 5 to that Act, after the words "in this paragraph" there shall be inserted the words "and in section 46 (5) of this Act".

6 In section 78 (4)(*b*) of the Finance Act 1976, the words "to the Board" and the words from "or" to "tax)" shall cease to have effect.

7 In section 114 (6) of that Act, for the words "the said section 37" there shall be substituted the words "section 37 of the said Act of 1975".

* * * * *

FINANCE (No 2) ACT 1983

An Act to grant certain duties, to alter other duties, and to amend the law relating to the National Debt and the Public Revenue, and to make further provision in connection with Finance.

[26 July 1983].

* * * * *

PART II

CAPITAL TRANSFER TAX

8 Reduction of tax

(1) Section 91(1) of the Finance Act 1982 (indexation of rate bands) shall not apply to chargeable transfers made in the year beginning with 6th April 1983.

(2) For the Tables in section 37(3) of the Finance Act 1975 there shall be substituted the Tables set out below.

FIRST TABLE

Portion of value		Rate of tax
Lower limit	Upper limit	Per cent
£	£	
0	60,000	Nil
60,000	80,000	30
80,000	110,000	35
110,000	140,000	40
140,000	175,000	45
175,000	220,000	50
220,000	270,000	55
270,000	700,000	60
700,000	1,325,000	65
1,325,000	2,650,000	70
2,650,000	—	75

SECOND TABLE

Portion of value		Rate of tax
Lower limit	Upper limit	Per cent
£	£	
0	60,000	Nil
60,000	80,000	15
80,000	110,000	17½
110,000	140,000	20
140,000	175,000	22½
175,000	220,000	25
220,000	270,000	30
270,000	700,000	35
700,000	1,325,000	40
1,325,000	2,650,000	45
2,650,000	—	50

(3) Subsection (2) above applies to any chargeable transfer made on or after 15th March 1983.

9 Gifts to charities

(1) In paragraph 10(1) of Schedule 6 to the Finance Act 1975 (exemption from tax for gifts to charities), paragraph (*b*) (which limits the exemption to £250,000 in respect of gifts on or within one year of the death of the transferor) shall cease to have effect.

(2) In section 117 of the Finance Act 1976 (modification of exemptions for loans) in subsection (5)—

(*a*) for the words "Paragraphs 10 and 11 (gifts to charities and" there shall be substituted the words "Paragraph 11 (gifts"; and

(*b*) for the words from "those paragraphs" to "13 (gifts" there shall be substituted the words "that paragraph and paragraphs 10, 12 and 13 (gifts to charities,".

(3) This section has effect in relation to transfers of value made on or after 15 March 1983.

10 Relief for business and agricultural property

(1) The appropriate percentage in the case of property falling within paragraph 3(1) (*bb*) of Schedule 10 to the Finance Act 1976 (relief for minority shareholdings in unquoted companies) shall be increased from 20 per cent to 30 per cent and accordingly in paragraph 2(1A) of that Schedule—

(*a*) paragraph (*b*) shall cease to have effect; and

(*b*) in paragraph (*c*), after the words "3(1)" there shall be inserted the words "(*bb*),".

(2) In sub-paragraphs (2) and (4) of paragraph 2 of Schedule 14 to the Finance Act 1981 (appropriate percentage in relation to relief for agricultural property) for the words "20 per cent" there shall, in each case, be substituted the words "30 per cent".

(3) This section has effect in relation to transfers of value made, and other events occurring, on or after 15th March 1983.

11 Payment of tax by instalments

(1) In paragraphs 13(1), 14(1) and 15 of Schedule 4 to the Finance Act 1975 (cases in which tax may be paid by instalments) for the words "at his option either by eight equal yearly instalments or by sixteen equal half-yearly instalments" there shall be substituted the words "by ten equal yearly instalments".

(2) In paragraph 13(3) of Schedule 4 (conditions applying in relation to transfers of certain shares) for the words "£5,000" there shall be substituted the words "£20,000".

(3) This section has effect in relation to chargeable transfers made on or after 15th March 1983.

12 Domicile

(1) Section 45(1)(*c*) of the Finance Act 1975 (which treats certain persons who have become domiciled in the Channel Islands or in the Isle of Man as domiciled in the United Kingdom) shall cease to have effect.

(2) This section has effect in relation to transfers of value made, and other events occurring, on or after 15th March 1983.

13 Burden of tax

(1) In section 28 of the Finance Act 1975 (burden of tax) the following subsections shall be substituted for subsection (1)—

> "(1) Where personal representatives are liable for tax on the value transferred by a chargeable transfer made on death, the tax shall be treated as part of the general testamentary and administration expenses of the estate, but only so far as it is attributable to the value of property in the United Kingdom which—
>
> (*a*) vests in the deceased's personal representatives; and
>
> (*b*) was not, immediately before the death, comprised in a settlement.
>
> The provision made by this subsection shall have effect subject to any contrary intention shown by the deceased in his will.
>
> (1A) Where any amount of tax paid by personal representatives on the value transferred by a chargeable transfer made on death does not fall to be borne as part of the general testamentary and administration expenses of the estate, that amount shall, where occasion requires, be repaid to them by the person in whom the property to the value of which the tax is attributable is vested."

(2) For subsection (8) of that section there shall be substituted—

> "(8) References in this section (except subsection (2)) to tax include references to interest on tax and, in subsections (3) to (5), to costs properly incurred in respect of tax."

(3) This section has effect where the death or other event on which tax is chargeable occurs on or after the day on which this Act is passed.

* * * * *

16 Short title, construction and repeals

(1) This Act may be cited as the Finance (No 2) Act 1983.

* * * * *

(3) Part II of this Act shall be construed as one with Part III of the Finance Act 1975.

(4) The enactments specified in Schedule 2 of this Act are hereby repealed to the extent specified in the third column of that Schedule, but subject to any provision at the end of any Part of that Schedule.

* * * * *

SCHEDULE 2

* * * * *

PART II

CAPITAL TRANSFER TAX

Chapter	Short Title	Extent of repeal
1925 c 23	The Administration of Estates Act 1925	In the First Schedule, paragraph 8 (*b*)
1955 c 24 (NI)	The Administration of Estates Act (Northern Ireland) 1955	In the First Schedule, paragraph 8 (*b*)
1975 c 7	The Finance Act 1975	In section 26(3), the words "10(1) (*b*) or", "given to a charity or property" and "charity or, as the case may be, the" In section 45, in subsection (1), paragraph (*c*) and the word "or" immediately preceding it, and subsections (2A) and (3) In Schedule 4, in paragraphs 12(3) and 19(2), the words "a charity or only" In Schedule 6, in paragraph 10(1), paragraph (*b*) and the word "and" immediately preceding it
1976 c 40	The Finance Act 1976	In Schedule 10, paragraph 2 (1A) (*b*)
1977 c 36	The Finance Act 1977	Section 49
1982 c 39	The Finance Act 1982	Section 92 (2)

1 The repeals in the Administration of Estates Act 1925 and the Administration of Estates Act (Northern Ireland) 1955 have effect in relation to deaths on or after the day on which this Act was passed.

2 The repeals of—

(*a*) subsections (1)(*c*), (2A) and (3) of section 45 of the Finance Act 1975,

(*b*) paragraph 2 (1A) (*b*) of Schedule 10 to the Finance Act 1976, and

(*c*) section 49 of the Finance Act 1977,

have effect in relation to transfers of value made, and other events occurring, on or after 15th March 1983.

3 The remaining repeals have effect in relation to transfers of value made on or after 15th March 1983.

FINANCE ACT 1984

An Act to grant certain duties, to alter other duties and to amend the law relating to the National Debt and the Public Revenue, and to make further provision in connection with Finance.

[26 July 1984].

* * * * *

PART III

CAPITAL TRANSFER TAX

101 Reduction of tax (1) Section 91(1)of the Finance Act 1982 (indexation of rate bands) shall not apply to chargeable transfers made in the year beginning with 6th April 1984.

(2) For the Tables in section 37(3) of the Finance Act 1975 there shall be substituted the Tables set out below.

FIRST TABLE

Portion of value		Rate of tax
Lower limit £	Upper limit £	Per cent.
0	64,000	Nil
64,000	85,000	30
85,000	116,000	35
116,000	148,000	40
148,000	185,000	45
185,000	232,000	50
232,000	285,000	55
285,000	—	60

SECOND TABLE

Portion of value		Rate of tax
Lower limit £	Upper limit £	Per cent.
0	64,000	Nil
64,000	85,000	15
85,000	116,000	17½
116,000	148,000	20
148,000	185,000	22½
185,000	232,000	25
232,000	285,000	27½
285,000	—	30

(3) Subsection (2) above applies to any chargeable transfer made on or after 13th March 1984.

102 Special discretionary trusts: excluded property (1) In section 113 of the Finance Act 1982 (charge to tax in respect of property leaving temporary charitable trusts), the following subsection shall be inserted after subsection (6) and will accordingly be applied by sections 114 (accumulation and maintenance trusts, 116 (property leaving employee trusts and newspaper trusts) and 118 (protective trusts and trusts for disabled persons) of that Act—

"(6A) Where the whole or part of the amount on which tax is charged under this section is attributable to property which was excluded property at any time during the relevant period then, in determining the rate at which tax is charged under this section in respect of that amount or part, no quarter throughout which that property was excluded property shall be counted."

(2) In subsection (7) of section 113 (which defines "relevant period" for the purposes of subsection (6)) for the words "subsection (6)" there shall be substituted the words "subsections (6) and (6A)".

(3) This section has effect in relation to events on or after 9th March 1982.

103 Discretionary trusts: distributions made within two years of testator's death (1) After subsection (1A) of section 47 of the Finance Act 1975 (certain distributions made within two years of testator's death to be treated as made under his will) there shall be inserted the following subsection—

"(1AA) This Part of this Act shall also apply as mentioned in subsection (1A)(*b*) above in any case where the circumstances are as mentioned in subsection (1A) but the event in question is one on which tax would be so chargeable apart from—

(*a*) section 115 of the Finance Act 1982 (property becoming subject to employee trusts);

(*b*) section 119 of that Act (property becoming held for charitable purposes or by exempt bodies); or

(*c*) paragraph 1(1) of Schedule 16 to that Act (property becoming comprised in maintenance funds for historic buildings)."

(2) This section has effect in relation to deaths occurring on or after 13th March 1984.

104 Property moving between settlements (1) In section 121 of the Finance Act 1982 (property moving between settlements), the following subsection shall be added at the end—

> "(3) Subsection (1) above does not apply where a reversionary interest in the property expectant on the termination of a qualifying interest in possession subsisting under the first settlement was settled on the trusts of the other settlement before 10th December 1981."

(2) In paragraph 3 of Schedule 7 to the Finance Act 1975 (certain government securities to be excluded property if person beneficially entitled is domiciled and ordinarily resident abroad) the following sub-paragraph shall be inserted after sub-paragraph (2A)—

> "(2AA) Sub-paragraph (2A) above does not apply where a reversionary interest in the property expectant on the termination of a qualifying interest in possession subsisting under the first settlement was settled on the trusts of the second settlement before 10th December 1981.".

(3) This section has effect in relation to events on or after 15th March 1983.

105 Adjustment of tax (1) In paragraph 23(3) of Schedule 4 to the Finance Act 1975 (adjustment of tax in cases of fraud, wilful default or neglect), for the words "a person liable for the tax, the period" there shall be substituted the words "any of the following—

(*a*) a person liable for the tax; and

(*b*) in the case of tax chargeable under Chapter II of Part IV of the Finance Act 1982, the person who is the settlor in relation to the settlement;

the period".

(2) With effect from 1st April 1983, subsection (8) of section 114 of the Finance Act 1976 (transfers reported late) shall cease to have effect.

(3) Subsection (1) above has effect in relation to any fraud, wilful default or neglect coming to the knowledge of the Board on or after 1st April 1983.

106 Recovery of tax (1) In Schedule 4 to the Finance Act 1975, after paragraph 22 there shall be inserted—

"22A.—In Scotland, tax and interest on tax may, without prejudice to any other remedy, and if the amount of the tax and interest does not exceed the sum for the time being specified in section 35(1)(*a*) of the Sheriff Courts (Scotland) Act 1971, be sued for and recovered in the sheriff court.

22B. An officer of the Board who is authorised by the Board to do so may address the court in any proceedings in a county court or sheriff court for the recovery of tax or interest on tax."

(2) After paragraph 36 of that Schedule there shall be inserted—

"36A. In any proceedings for the recovery of tax or interest on tax, a certificate by an officer of the Board—

(*a*) that the tax or interest is due, or

(*b*) that, to the best of his knowledge and belief, it has not been paid.

shall be sufficient evidence that the sum mentioned in the certificate is due or, as the case may be, unpaid; and a document purporting to be such a certificate shall be deemed to be such a certificate unless the contrary is proved."

107 Relief for stud farms (1) For the purposes of Schedule 14 to the Finance Act 1981 (capital transfer tax: relief for agricultural property) the breeding and rearing of horses on a stud farm and the grazing of horses in connection with those activities shall be taken to be agriculture and any buildings used in connection with those activities to be farm buildings.

"(2) In paragraph 12 of Schedule 10 to the Finance Act 1975 (farm cottages) the existing provisions shall become sub paragraph (1) and at the end there shall be inserted—

"(2) Expressions used in sub-paragraph (1) above and in Schedule 14 to the Finance Act 1981 have the same meaning in that sub-paragraph as in that Schedule."

(3) In section 97 of the Finance Act 1981 (grant of tenancies of agricultural property) for subsection (2) there shall be substituted—

"(2) Expressions used in subsection (1) above and in Schedule 14 to this Act have the same meaning in that subsection as in that Schedule."

(4) This section has effect in relation to transfers of value and other events occurring on or after 10th March 1981.

108 Pre-consolidation amendments Schedule 21 to this

Act (which contains amendments designed to facilitate, or otherwise desirable in connection with, the consolidation of the law relating to capital transfer tax) shall have effect.

* * * * *

127 Special and General Commissioners (1) Schedule 22 to this Act shall have effect for the purpose of making provision in relation to the Special and General Commissioners.

(2) This section and Part XIII of Schedule 23 to this Act shall come into operation on such day as the Lord Chancellor may by order made by statutory instrument appoint, and different days may be so appointed for different provisions and for different purposes.

128 Short title, interpretation, construction and repeals (1) This Act may be cited as the Finance Act 1984.

* * * * *

(4) Part III of this Act shall be construed as one with Part III of the Finance Act 1975.

* * * * *

(6) The enactments specified in Schedule 23 to this Act are hereby repealed to the extent specified in the third column of that Schedule, but subject to any provision at the end of any Part of that Schedule.

* * * * *

SCHEDULE 14

BENEFICIARY'S LIABILITY FOR TAX ON GAINS OF NON-RESIDENT TRUSTEES

Consequential relief from C.T.T.

16. In any case where—

(*a*) payment of any amount of capital gains tax is postponed by virtue of this Schedule, and

(*b*) any of that tax becomes payable in accordance with paragraph 11 above by reason of the receipt of a capital payment by a close relative of the beneficiary, as mentioned in sub-paragraph (3) of that paragraph, and

(*c*) all or part of the tax becoming so payable is paid by the close relative,

the payment by the close relative shall be treated for the purposes of capital transfer tax as made in satisfaction of a liability of his.

* * * * *

SCHEDULE 21

CAPITAL TRANSFER TAX: PRE-CONSOLIDATION AMENDMENTS

The Finance Act 1975

1. In section 22(4) of the Finance Act 1975 (in this Schedule referred to as "the 1975 Act")—

(*a*) for the words from the beginning to "his death" there shall be substituted the words "In determining for the purposes of this Part of this Act the value of the estate, immediately before his death, of a person whose spouse (or former spouse) died before 13th November 1974"; and

(*b*) for the words "that death" there shall be substituted the words "the later death".

2. In section 25(10) of the 1975 Act, after the word "section" there shall be inserted the words "(except subsection (8))".

3. In section 26(2) of the 1975 Act—

(*a*) the words from the beginning to "respectively, and" shall cease to have effect; and

(*b*) at the end, there shall be added the words "or by virtue of paragraph 24(2) of Schedule 5 to this Act".

4. In section 45(1) of the 1975 Act, after the words "as domiciled in the United Kingdom" there shall be inserted the words "(and not elsewhere)"; and section 51(3) of that Act shall cease to have effect.

5. In section 51(1) of the 1975 Act—

(*a*) the definition of "enactment" shall cease to have effect; and

(*b*) after the definition of "Inland Revenue charge" there shall be inserted—

"'land' includes buildings and other structures, land

covered with water, and any estate, interest, easement, servitude or right in or over land; but does not include any estate, interest or right by way of mortgage or other security;".

6. In paragraph 6(6) of Schedule 4 to the 1975 Act, for the words following "including references" there shall be substituted the words "to—

(*a*) disposals on which tax is chargeable under paragraph 2 of Schedule 9 to this Act.

(*b*) chargeable events by reference to which tax is chargeable under section 78 of the Finance Act 1976,

(*c*) occasions on which tax is chargeable under section 82 of the Finance Act 1976 or under Chapter II of Part IV of the Finance Act 1982,

or to the amounts on which tax is then chargeable."

7. In paragraph 14(2) of Schedule 4 to the 1975 Act, for the words "value of an interest" there shall be substituted the words "net value of an interest".

8. In paragraph 19(4) of Schedule 4 to the 1975 Act, the words "to any person" and the words "of that person" shall cease to have effect.

9. Paragraph 44 of Schedule 4 to the 1975 Act shall cease to have effect.

10. In paragraph 1(8) of Schedule 5 to the 1975 Act, for the words "and section 25(3)(*d*) of this Act" there shall be substituted the words ", sections 22(2) and (3), 24(3) and 25(3)(*d*) of this Act and sections 93 and 94".

11. In paragraph 4(7) of Schedule 5 to the 1975 Act, after the words "surviving spouse" there shall be inserted the words "(or surviving former spouse)".

12. In paragraph 17(3)(*b*) of Schedule 5 to the 1975 Act, for the words "this Schedule and of Chapter II of Part IV of the Finance Act 1982" there shall be substituted the words "this Part of this Act (except subsection (3) of section 23 and section 20(4) so far as relating to that subsection)".

13. In paragraph 22(1) of Schedule 5 to the 1975 Act, for the words "this Schedule" there shall be substituted the words "this Part of this Act".

14. (1) Paragraph 24 of Schedule 5 to the 1975 Act shall be amended as follows.

(2) In sub-paragraph (1), for paragraph (*a*) there shall be substituted the following paragraphs—

"(*a*) the reference in subsection (2) of that section to subsection (1) shall have effect as including a reference to sub-paragraph (2) below;

(*aa*) subsection (3) of that section shall apply in relation to tax chargeable by virtue of sub-paragraph (2) below as it applies in relation to tax chargeable under subsection (1) of that section;".

(3) In sub-paragraph (5), for the words "this Schedule and of Chapter II of Part IV of the Finance Act 1982" there shall be substituted the words "this Part of this Act (except subsection (3) of section 23 and section 20(4) so far as relating to that subsection)".

15. In paragraph 4(2)(*b*) of Schedule 7 to the 1975 Act, for the words "which is, or forms part of, a colony, protectorate, protected state or United Kingdom trust territory" there shall be substituted the words "which, at the time when the fund was established, was, or formed part of, a colony (within the meaning of Schedule 1 to the Interpretation Act 1978), protectorate, protected state or United Kingdom trust territory".

16. In paragraph 1(1) of Schedule 10 to the 1975 Act, for the words "a transferor's estate" there shall be substituted the words "a person's estate".

17. In paragraph 5(1)(*b*) of Schedule 10 to the 1975 Act, for the word "by" there shall be substituted the word "for".

The Finance Act 1976

20. In section 76(3)(*b*) of the Finance Act 1976, the words from "or the value" to the end shall cease to have effect.

21. In section 105 of the Finance Act 1976, subsections (3) and (4) shall cease to have effect.

22. In section 123(2) of the Finance Act 1976, after the words "shall carry interest" there shall be inserted the words "(which shall not constitute income for any tax purposes)".

The Finance Act 1980

23. In Schedule 15 to the Finance Act 1980—

(*a*) in paragraphs 2A, 5 and 6, for the word "previous" there shall be substituted the word "other"; and

(*b*) in paragraphs 5 and 6, after the words "by that reduction" there shall be inserted the words "(or by the most recent of those reductions)".

The Finance Act 1982

24. In section 94(6) of the Finance Act 1982, the words from "and, in" to the end shall cease to have effect.

25. In sections 120(1), 121(1) and (2) and 123 of the Finance Act 1982, after the words "for the purposes of this Chapter" there shall be inserted the words ", of sections 93 and 94 above and of sections 81, 82 and 82A of the Finance Act 1976".

26. In sections 122(1) and 124 of the Finance Act 1982, after the words "for the purposes of this Chapter" there shall be inserted the words "and of sections 93 and 94 above".

SCHEDULE 22

SPECIAL AND GENERAL COMMISSIONERS

* * * * *

Fee for statement of case

6. In section 56(3) of the Act of 1970 and paragraph 10(2) of Schedule 4 to the Finance Act 1975 (fee for statement of case for opinion of High Court) for "£1" there shall be substituted "£25".

* * * * *

SCHEDULE 23

REPEALS

* * * * *

PART IX

CAPITAL TRANSFER TAX

Chapter	Short title	Extent of repeal
1975 c. 7.	The Finance Act 1975.	In section 26(2), the words from the beginning to "respectively, and". In section 51(1), the definition of "enactment". Section 51(3). In Schedule 4, in paragraph 19(4), the words "to any person" and the words "of that person". In Schedule 4, paragraph 44.
1976 c. 40.	The Finance Act 1976.	In section 76(3)(*b*), the words from "or the value" onwards. Section 105(3) and (4). Section 114(8). In Schedule 11, paragraph 2.
1982 c. 39.	The Finance Act 1982.	In section 94(6), the words from "and, in" onwards. In Schedule 17, paragraphs 9, 18 and 28.

The repeal of section 114(8) of the Finance Act 1976 has effect as from 1st April 1983.

The Estate Duty (Interest on Unpaid Duty) Order 1982 (SI 1982 No 1584)

The Treasury, in exercise of the powers conferred on them by section 30 of the Finance Act 1970, hereby make the following Order:—

1 This order may be cited as the Estate Duty (Interest on Unpaid Duty) Order 1982 and shall come into operation on 1st December 1982.

2 The rate of interest payable under the following enactments, namely—

(*a*) section 18 of the Finance Act 1896;

(*b*) section 61(5) of the Finance (1909–10) Act 1910 as amended by section 9 of the Finance Act 1912; and

(*c*) section 17(3) of the Law of Property Act 1925 and section 73(6) of the Land Registration Act 1925.

shall, as regards interest accruing on or after 1st December 1982, be 6 per cent. instead of 9 per cent., per annum.

3 Section 8(9) of the Finance Act 1894 shall, as regards interest accruing on or after 1st December 1982, have effect with the substitution of the word "six" for the word "nine".

The Capital Transfer Tax (Interest on Unpaid Tax) Order 1982 (SI 1982 No 1585)

The Treasury, in exercise of the powers conferred on them by paragraph 19 of Schedule 4 to the Finance Act 1975, hereby make the following Order:—

1 This Order may be cited as the Capital Transfer Tax (Interest on Unpaid Tax) Order 1982 and shall come into operation on 1st December 1982.

2 The prescribed rate of interest on any unpaid tax on which interest is payable under paragraph 19(1) of Schedule 4 to the Finance Act 1975 shall be:

(*a*) if the chargeable transfer was made on death, 6 per cent., instead of 9 per cent., per annum

(*b*) in any other case, 8 per cent., instead of 12 per cent., per annum.

The Capital Transfer Tax (Delivery of Accounts) (No 3) Regulations 1983 (SI 1983 No 1039)

The Commissioners of Inland Revenue, in exercise of the powers conferred on them by section 94(1) of the Finance Act 1980, hereby make the following Regulations:

Citation, commencement and extent

1 These Regulations may be cited as the Capital Transfer Tax (Delivery of Accounts (No 3) Regulations 1983 and shall come into operation on 1st September 1983.

2 These Regulations do not extend to Scotland or Northern Ireland.

Interpretation

3 In these Regulations "the Principal Regulations" means The Capital Transfer Tax (Delivery of Accounts) Regulations 1981.

Amendments to Principal Regulations

4 In Regulation 3 of the Principal Regulations

(*a*) in paragraph (*b*) for "£25,000" there shall be substituted "£40,000";

(*b*) in paragraph (*c*) for "£1,000" there shall be substituted "£2,000";

(*c*) in paragraph (*d*) for "1st April 1981" there shall be substituted "1st April 1983".

The Capital Transfer Tax (Delivery of Accounts) (Scotland) (No 2) Regulations 1983 (SI 1983 No 1040)

The Commissioners of Inland Revenue, in exercise of the powers conferred on them by section 94(1) of the Finance Act 1980, hereby make the following Regulations:

Citation, commencement and extent

1 These Regulations may be cited as the Capital Transfer Tax (Delivery of Accounts) (Scotland) (No 2) Regulations 1983 and shall come into operation on 1 September 1983.

2 These Regulations extend to Scotland only.

Interpretation

3 In these Regulations 'the Principal Regulations' means The Capital Transfer Tax (Delivery of Accounts) (Scotland) Regulations 1981.

Amendments to Principal Regulations

4 In Regulation 3 of the Principal Regulations

(*a*) in paragraph (*b*) for '£25,000' there shall be substituted '£40,000';

(*b*) in paragraph (*c*) for '£1,000' there shall be substituted '£2,000';

(*c*) in paragraph (*d*) for '1st April 1981' there shall be substituted '1st April 1983'.

The Capital Transfer Tax (Delivery of Accounts) (Northern Ireland) (No 2) Regulations 1983 (SI 1983 No 1911)

The Commissioners of Inland Revenue, in exercise of the powers conferred on them by section 94(1) of the Finance Act 1980, hereby make the following Regulations:

Citation, commencement and extent

1 The Regulations may be cited as the Capital Transfer Tax (Delivery of Accounts) (Northern Ireland) (No 2) Regulations 1983 and shall come into operation on 1st February 1984.

2 These Regulations extend to Northern Ireland only.

Interpretation

3 In these Regulations "the Principal Regulations" means The Capital Transfer Tax (Delivery of Accounts) (Northern Ireland) Regulations 1981.

Amendments to Principal Regulations

4 In Regulation 3 of the Principal Regulations

(*a*) in paragraph (*b*) for "£25,000" there shall be substituted "£40,000";

(*b*) in paragraph (*c*) for "£1,000" there shall be substituted "£2,000";

(*c*) in paragraph (*d*) for "1st April 1981" there shall be substituted "1st April 1983".

The OECD Model Double Taxation Convention on Estates and Inheritances and on Gifts (1982)

SUMMARY OF THE CONVENTION

TERMINAL CLAUSE

TITLE OF THE CONVENTION

Convention between (State A) and (State B) for the avoidance of double taxation with respect to taxes on estates and inheritances and on gifts.

PREAMBLE OF THE CONVENTION

Note: The Preamble of the Convention shall be drafted in accordance with the constitutional procedure of both Contracting States.

Chapter I

SCOPE OF THE CONVENTION

1 Estates, inheritances and gifts covered

This Convention shall apply:

(*a*) to estates and inheritances where the deceased was domiciled, at the time of his death, in one or both of the Contracting States, and

(*b*) to gifts where the donor was domiciled, at the time of the gift, in one or both of the Contracting States.

2 Taxes covered

(1) This Convention shall apply to taxes on estates and inheritances and on gifts imposed on behalf of a Contracting State or of its political subdivisions or local authorities, irrespective of the manner in which they are levied.

(2) There shall be regarded as taxes on estates and inheritances taxes imposed by reason of death in the form of taxes on the *corpus* of the estate, of taxes on inheritances, of transfer duties, or of taxes on *donationes mortis causa*. There shall be regarded as taxes on gifts taxes imposed on transfers *inter vivos* only because such transfers are made for no, or less than full, consideration.

(3) The existing taxes to which the Convention shall apply are:

(*a*) (in State A) ....

(*b*) (In State B) ....

(4) The Convention shall apply also to any identical or substantially similar taxes which are imposed after the date of signature of the Convention in addition to, or in place of, the existing taxes. At the end of each year, the competent authorities of the Contracting States shall notify each other of changes which have been made in their respective taxation laws.

Chapter II

DEFINITIONS

3 General definitions

(1) For the purposes of this Convention, unless the context otherwise requires:

(*a*) the term "property which forms part of the estate of, or of a gift made by, a person domiciled in a Contracting State" includes any property the devolution or transfer of which, under the law of a Contracting State, is liable to a tax covered by the Convention;

(*b*) the term "competent authority" means;

(i) (in State A) ....

(ii) (in State B) ....

(2) As regards the application of the Convention by a Contracting State, any term not defined therein shall, unless the context otherwise requires, have the meaning which it has under the law of that State concerning the taxes to which the Convention applies.

4 Fiscal domicile

(1) For the purposes of this Convention, the term "person domiciled in a Contracting State" means any person whose estate or whose gift, under the law of that State, is liable to tax therein by reason of the domicile, residence or place of management of that person or any other criterion of a similar nature. However, this term does not include any person whose estate or whose gift is liable to tax in that State only in respect of property situated therein.
(2) Where by reason of the provisions of paragraph (1) an individual is domiciled in both Contracting States, then his status shall be determined as follows:

(*a*) he shall be deemed to be domiciled in the State in which he has a permanent home available to him; if he has a permanent home available to him in both States, he shall be deemed to be domiciled in the State with which his personal and economic relations are closer (centre of vital interests);

(*b*) if the State in which he has his centre of vital interests cannot be determined, or if he has not a permanent home available to him in either State, he shall be deemed to be domiciled in the State in which he has an habitual abode;

(*c*) if he has an habitual abode in both States or in neither of them, he shall be deemed to be domiciled in the State of which he is a national;

(*d*) if he is a national of both States or of neither of them, the competent authorities of the Contracting States shall settle the question by mutual agreement.

(3) Where by reason of the provisions of paragraph (1) a person other than an individual is domiciled in both Contracting States, then it shall be deemed to be domiciled in the State in which its place of effective management is situated.

Chapter III

TAXING RULES

5 Immovable property

(1) Immovable property which forms part of the estate of, or of a gift made by, a person domiciled in a Contracting State and which is situated in the other Contracting State may be taxed in that other State.
(2) The term "immovable property" shall have the meaning which it has under the law of the Contracting State in which the property in question is situated. The term shall in any case include property accessory to immovable property, livestock and equipment used in agriculture and forestry, rights to which the provisions of general law respecting landed property apply, usufruct of immovable property and rights to variable or fixed payments as consideration for the working of, or the right to work, mineral deposits, sources and other natural resources; ships, boats and aircraft shall not be regarded as immovable property.
(3) The provisions of paragraph (1) shall also apply to immovable property of an enterprise and to immovable property used for the performance of professional services or other activities of an independent character.

6 Movable property of a permanent establishment or a fixed base

(1) Movable property of an enterprise which forms part of the estate of, or of a gift made by, a person domiciled in a Contracting State, which is the business property of a permanent establishment situated in the other Contracting State, may be taxed in that other State.
(2) For the purposes of this Convention, the term "permanent establishment" means a fixed place of business through which the business of an enterprise is wholly or partly carried on.
(3) The term "permanent establishment" includes especially:
(*a*) a place of management;

(*b*) a branch;
(*c*) an office;
(*d*) a factory;
(*e*) a workshop; and
(*f*) a mine, an oil or gas well, a quarry or any other place of extraction of natural resources.

(4) A building site or construction or installation project constitutes a permanent establishment only if it lasts more than twelve months.

(5) Notwithstanding the preceding provisions of this Article, the term "permanent establishment" shall be deemed not to include:
(*a*) the use of facilities solely for the purpose of storage, display or delivery of goods or merchandise belonging to the enterprise;
(*b*) the maintenance of a stock of goods or merchandise belonging to the enterprise solely for the purpose of storage, display or delivery;
(*c*) the maintenance of a stock of goods or merchandise belonging to the enterprise solely for the purpose of processing by another enterprise;
(*d*) the maintenance of a fixed place of business solely for the purpose of purchasing goods or merchandise, or of collecting information, for the enterprise;
(*e*) the maintenance of a fixed place of business solely for the purpose of carrying on for the enterprise any other activity of a preparatory or auxiliary character; or
(*f*) the maintenance of a fixed place of business solely for any combination of activities mentioned in subparagraphs (*a*) to (*e*), provided that the overall activity of the fixed place of business resulting from this combination is of a preparatory or auxiliary character.

(6) Movable property which forms part of the estate of, or of a gift made by, a person domiciled in a Contracting State, used for the performance of professional services or other activities of an independent character and pertaining to a fixed base situated in the other Contracting State, may be taxed in that other State.

7 Other property

Property, wherever situated, which forms part of the estate of, or of a gift made by, a person domiciled in a Contracting State, and not dealt with in Articles 5 and 6, shall be taxable only in that State.

8 Deduction of debts

(1) Debts especially secured on any property referred to in Article 5 shall be deducted from the value of that property. Debts, not being especially secured on any property referred to in Article 5, which are represented by the acquisition, conversion, repair or upkeep of any such property, shall be deducted from the value of that property.
(2) Subject to the provisions of paragraph (1), debts pertaining to a permanent establishment referred to in paragraph (1) of Article 6, or to a fixed base referred to in paragraph (6) of Article 6, shall be deducted from the value of the permanent establishment or the fixed base as the case may be.
(3) Other debts shall be deducted from the value of property to which the provisions of Article 7 apply.
(4) If a debt exceeds the value of the property from which it is deductible in a Contracting State, according to the provisions of paragraphs (1) or (2), the excess shall be deducted from the value of any other property taxable in that State.
(5) Any excess still remaining in one Contracting State after the deductions referred to in paragraphs (3) or (4) shall be deducted from the value of the property liable to tax in the other Contracting State.
(6) Where the provisions of paragraphs (1) to (5) would oblige one Contracting State to deduct debts to an extent greater than that provided for under its law, those provisions shall apply only to the extent that the other Contracting State is not obliged to deduct the same debts under its own law.

Chapter IV

METHODS FOR ELIMINATING DOUBLE TAXATION

9A Exemption method

(1) The Contracting State in which the deceased was domiciled at his death, or the donor was domiciled at the time of the gift, shall exempt from tax any property which, in relation to the same event and in accordance with the provisions of this Convention, may be taxed in the other Contracting State.
(2) The former Contracting State shall also exempt from tax any property which, in relation to a previous gift and in accordance with the provisions of the Convention, may have been taxed in the

other Contracting State. That former State, however, shall not exempt from tax any property which was taxable in that State in accordance with the provisions of Articles 5 or 6 of the Convention.
(3) In each case the former Contracting State may take the exempted property into account in calculating the amount of tax on any remaining property.

9B Credit method

(1) The Contracting State in which the deceased was domiciled at his death, or the donor was domiciled at the time of the gift, shall allow as a deduction from the tax calculated according to its law an amount equal to the tax paid in the other Contracting State on any property which, in relation to the same event and in accordance with the provisions of this Convention, may be taxed in that other State.
(2) The former Contracting State shall also allow as a deduction from such tax an amount equal to the tax which has been paid in the other Contracting State on a previous gift in accordance with the provisions of the Convention to the extent that such a deduction has not been allowed under the provisions of paragraph (1) at the time of that gift. That former State, however, shall not allow a deduction in respect of tax paid on property which was taxable in that State in accordance with the provisions of Articles 5 or 6 of the Convention.
(3) The deductions referred to in paragraphs (1) and (2) shall not, however, exceed that part of the tax of the former Contracting State, as computed before any deduction is made, which is attributable to the property in respect of which the deduction is to be allowed.

Chapter V

SPECIAL PROVISIONS

10 Non-discrimination

(1) Nationals of a Contracting State, wherever they are domiciled, shall not be subjected in the other Contracting State to any taxation, or any requirement connected therewith, which is other or more burdensome than the taxation and connected requirements to which nationals of that other State in the same circumstances are or may be subjected.

(2) The term "nationals" means:

(*a*) all individuals possessing the nationality of a Contracting State;

(*b*) all legal persons, partnerships and associations deriving their status as such from the law in force in a Contracting State.

(3) Stateless persons who are domiciled in a Contracting State shall not be subjected in either Contracting State to any taxation, or any requirement connected therewith, which is other or more burdensome than the taxation and connected requirements to which nationals of the State concerned in the same circumstances are or may be subjected.

(4) The provisions of this Article shall, notwithstanding the provisions of Article 2, apply to taxes of every kind and description.

11 Mutual agreement procedure

(1) Where a person considers that the actions of one or both of the Contracting States result or will result for him in taxation not in accordance with the provisions of this Convention, he may, irrespective of the remedies provided by the domestic laws of those States, present his case to the competent authority of either Contracting State. The case must be presented within three years from the first notification of the action resulting in taxation not in accordance with the provisions of the Convention.

(2) The competent authority, if the objection appears to it to be justified and if it is not itself able to arrive at a satisfactory solution, shall endeavour to resolve the case by mutual agreement with the competent authority of the other Contracting State, with a view to the avoidance of taxation which is not in accordance with the provisions of the Convention. Any agreement reached shall be implemented notwithstanding any time limits in the domestic laws of the Contracting States.

(3) The competent authorities of the Contracting States shall endeavour to resolve by mutual agreement any difficulties or doubts arising as to the interpretation or application of the Convention. They may also consult together for the elimination of double taxation in cases not provided for in the Convention.

(4) The competent authorities of the Contracting States may communicate with each other directly for the purpose of reaching an agreement in the sense of the preceding paragraphs. When it seems advisable in order to reach agreement to have an oral exchange of opinions, such exchange may take place through a

Commission consisting of representatives of the competent authorities of the Contracting States.

12 Exchange of information

(1) The competent authorities of the Contracting States shall exchange such information as is necessary for carrying out the provisions of this Convention or of the domestic laws of the Contracting States concerning taxes covered by the Convention insofar as the taxation thereunder is not contrary to the Convention. The exchange of information is not restricted by Article 1. Any information received by a Contracting State shall be treated as secret in the same manner as information obtained under the domestic laws of that State and shall be disclosed only to persons or authorities (including courts and administrative bodies) involved in the assessment or collection of, the enforcement or prosecution in respect of, or the determination of appeals in relation to, the taxes covered by the Convention. Such persons or authorities shall use the information only for such purposes. They may disclose the information in public court proceedings or in judicial decisions.

(2) In no case shall the provisions of paragraph (1) be construed so as to impose on a Contracting State the obligation:

- (*a*) to carry out administrative measures at variance with the laws or administrative practice of that or of the other State;
- (*b*) to supply information which is not obtainable under the laws, or in the normal course of the administration, of that or of the other State;
- (*c*) to supply information which would disclose any trade, business, industrial, commercial or professional secret or trade process, or information, the disclosure of which would be contrary to public policy (ordre public).

13 Diplomatic agents and consular officers

Nothing in this Convention shall affect the fiscal privileges of diplomatic agents or consular officers under the general rules of international law or under the provisions of special agreements.

14 Territorial extension

(1) This Convention may be extended, either in its entirety or with any necessary modifications, [to any part of the territory of

(State A) or of (State B) which is specifically excluded from the application of the Convention or] to any State or territory for whose international relations (State A) or (State B) is responsible, which imposes taxes substantially similar in character to those to which the Convention applies. Any such extension shall take effect from such date and subject to such modifications and conditions, including conditions as to termination, as may be specified and agreed between the Contracting States in notes to be exchanged through diplomatic channels or in any other manner in accordance with their constitutional procedures.
(2) Unless otherwise agreed by both Contracting States, the termination of the Convention by one of them under Article 16 shall also terminate, in the manner provided for in that Article, the application of the Convention [to any part of the territory of (State A) or of (State B) or] to any State or territory to which it has been extended under this Article.

Note: The words between square brackets are of relevance when, by special provision, a part of the territory of a Contracting State is excluded from the application of the Convention.

Chapter VI

FINAL PROVISIONS

15 Entry into force

(1) This Convention shall be ratified and the instruments of ratification shall be exchanged at .... as soon as possible.
(2) The Convention shall enter into force upon the exchange of instruments of ratification and its provisions shall have effect:
(*a*) (in State A) ....
(*b*) (in State B) ....

16 Termination

This Convention shall remain in force until terminated by a Contracting State. Either Contracting State may terminate the Convention, through diplomatic channels, by giving notice of termination at least six months before the end of any calendar year after the year .... In such event, the Convention shall cease to have effect:

(*a*) (in State A) ....

(*b*) (in State B) ....

TERMINAL CLAUSE

Note: The terminal clause shall be drafted in accordance with the constitutional procedure of both Contracting States.

INDEX